#Think

Critical Thinking about Social Problems

Vera Kennedy
Romney Norwood
Matthew Jendian

Kendall Hunt
publishing company

Book Team
Chairman and Chief Executive Officer   Mark C. Falb
President and Chief Operating Officer   Chad M. Chandlee
Vice President, Higher Education   David L. Tart
Director of Publishing Partnerships   Paul B. Carty
Development/Product Supervisor   Lynnette M. Rogers
Vice President, Operations   Timothy J. Beitzel
Permissions Coordinator   Caroline Kieler
Cover Designer   Faith Walker

Editing Contributions given by Matthew Ari Jendian.

Cover images © Shutterstock, Inc.
Cover idea credited to West Hills College Lemoore student, Tara Machado.

Kendall Hunt
publishing company

www.kendallhunt.com
Send all inquiries to:
4050 Westmark Drive
Dubuque, IA 52004-1840

Brief Contents

Contents

Preface

Critical Thinking about Social Problems is an interactive teaching tool to inspire student engagement and learning. The text focuses on developing critical thinking competencies by examining social problems to improve analytical and investigative skills. Exercises (i.e., sociological applications) are embedded throughout the text and are designed to enthuse reflective thinking, social literacy and responsibility, and civic involvement.

The text is designed to encourage active learning requiring students to seek out and practice critical thinking. Information and data presented in modules give instructional facilitators and learners the ability to choose topics of interest to study and examine. Each module contains several current and emerging social issues to employ critical thinking; however, modules are designed with the flexibility to add or incorporate instructor and student content as needed or desired. This format also allows instructors and students the ability to change sociological application topics while exploring the discussion or critical thinking questions provided. Though the text is designed with the flexibility to customize the learning experience, Modules 1 and 2 contain critical thinking and sociological fundamentals required to build competencies and should be reviewed prior to investigating social issue content modules.

Vera Kennedy

Vera Guerrero Kennedy was born and raised in San Joaquin Valley, California. She received a B.A. in sociology (1995) and M.P.A. in political science with an emphasis in public administration (1999) from Fresno State and a doctorate in education (Ed.D.) with an emphasis in curriculum and instruction from Argosy University (2012). She is certified by the National Grant Writers Association as a Senior Certified Grants Specialist and Certified Grants Reviewer.

Dr. Kennedy is a tenured faculty at West Hills College Lemoore and Lecturer at Fresno State. Her research publications include *The Influence of Cultural Capital on Hispanic Student College Graduation Rates* and *Improving Undergraduate Student Understanding of Social Research through Service Learning.* She serves on the Merlot Sociology Editorial Board and was an e-textbook reviewer in 2015 for the California OER Council (Cool4Ed). She was awarded West Hills Community College District Innovation Awards in 2015 and 2016 for her application of information, imagination, and initiative in transforming curriculum and instruction by integrating open education resources and e-devices.

Dr. Kennedy was invited to participate in the eScholars program at Fresno State (2012) to prepare and move beyond basic online course work by developing creative and engaging learning experiences for students. In 2010 she received the National Institute for Staff and Organizational Development (NISOD) Excellence Award and was recognized by the West Hills College Lemoore Team TEACH program as an All-star in Teaching. She received a Certificate of Recognition for the 7th Annual Outstanding Leadership Awards in Honor of Hispanic Heritage Month from the California State Assembly (2005) for work in applied social research, organizational development, and capacity building in partnership with public and non-profit agencies.

Before teaching full-time, Dr. Kennedy worked as the Juvenile Justice Services Coordinator for the Fresno Superior Court and assisted in the establishment and facilitation of the Juvenile Mental Health Court for Fresno County. She owned and operated a private consulting firm for six years. From 1999–2002, she served as the Associate Director for the Central California Center for Health and Human Services at Fresno State. Dr. Kennedy served on the Board of Directors for Comprehensive Youth Services, a child abuse prevention agency for eight years, and was appointed by the Fresno County Board of Supervisors to serve on the Fresno County Foster Care Oversight Committee for six years. She also served as a member of the Fresno County Human Resources Advisory Board responsible for reviewing and recommending local grant funding administered by the County of Fresno.

She and her husband, Greg, reside in Fresno, California with their "fur" kids, Woofers and Osa.

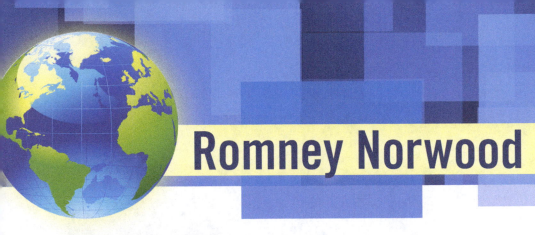

Romney Norwood

Romney Simone Norwood was born and raised in Shreveport, Louisiana. She received a B.S. in broadcast journalism (1995) from Boston University, an M.A. in sociology (1996) from Arizona State University and a dual title Ph.D. in sociology and demography (2001) from The Pennsylvania State University. Dr. Norwood is a tenured faculty member at Perimeter College at Georgia State University. Her research publications include *Marital Strain and Depressive Symptoms among African Americans* (with Keith) and *Ethnic Differences in Public Participation: The Role of Conflict Communication Styles and Sense of Community* (with Bernstein) which received the Top Paper Award at the 2007 annual International Public Relations Research Conference.

Dr. Norwood has also used her research skills in applied settings such as the Centers for Disease Control and Prevention (CDC,) where her training as a behavioral scientist was utilized to help implement a new schedule for administering the polio vaccine to children in the United States. For her work with the National Immunization Program (NIP) at the CDC, Dr. Norwood received a certificate of commendation for the development of the scientific and programmatic basis for the introduction of a sequential schedule for the prevention of vaccine-associated poliomyelitis in the United States and was recognized for Outstanding Achievement in Public Health by the U.S. Department of Health and Human Services.

Dr. Norwood is committed to offering her students opportunities to engage with their local communities and in 2012 she received the Faculty Fellow Award at Perimeter College which provides resources to support and encourage the development of service learning opportunities for students. Dr. Norwood has a long record of engaging in community service. She volunteers regularly with numerous organizations in the Atlanta metropolitan area and for 12 years she has volunteered monthly with Ten Thousand Villages, a fair trade organization with the goal of ensuring that artisans from developing countries are paid fairly for the handcrafted items that they produce and sell to sustain their families. Dr. Norwood served as board member for Ten Thousand Villages—Atlanta from 2007–2012.

She and her husband Louis reside in Atlanta, Georgia with their son Asher "the Dasher."

Matthew Jendian

Matthew Ari Jendian was born and raised in Fresno and received his B.A. in sociology and minor degrees in psychology and Armenian Studies from Fresno State (1991) and his M.A. (1995) and Ph.D. (2001) in Sociology from University of Southern California (USC).

Dr. Jendian is founding director of the Humanics Program at Fresno State and serves as a tenured Full Professor and Chair of sociology. He is the author of several peer-reviewed journal articles as well as *Becoming American, Remaining Ethnic* (LFB Scholarly Publishing, 2008), and he was honored in *Menk*, an encyclopedia of biographies of prominent Armenian scholars.

Dr. Jendian is the recipient of several honors, including the 2012 President's Award of Excellence presented by the University Advisory Board at Fresno State in recognition of his integrity, leadership and commitment to the university and community, the 2008 "Provost's Award for Faculty Service," the 2016 "Together We Win Award" in recognition of his role in civic engagement, the 2014 "Trailblazer for Prosperity" Award from Southeast Fresno Community & Economic Development Association, the 2007 Social Action Award from Temple Beth Israel, and the 2007 "Amigo Award" presented by Vida en El Valle to "a non-Latino individual or organization that has worked tirelessly on behalf of the Latino community." He was nominated for the 2009 California Campus Compact Cone Award for Excellence & Leadership in Cultivating Community Partnerships, was selected as part of the first cohort of the Irvine Foundation's New Leadership Network, and has written and received national and federal grants to develop curricula that engage university students in capacity-building work with Community Benefit Organizations (CBOs) in Central California.

Dr. Jendian has served as a board member for several CBOs, including Nonprofit Leadership Alliance (formerly American Humanics, Inc.), Buchanan Babe Ruth Baseball Association, Inc., Fresno Nonprofit Advancement Council, Fresno Housing Alliance, Regenerate California Innovation (formerly Relational Culture Institute), and Fresno Metro Ministry and as an external evaluator with local and multinational CBOs, including Porterville College and Armenian General Benevolent Union.

He and his wife, Pam, reside in Clovis, California with their two sons, Joshua and Nicholas.

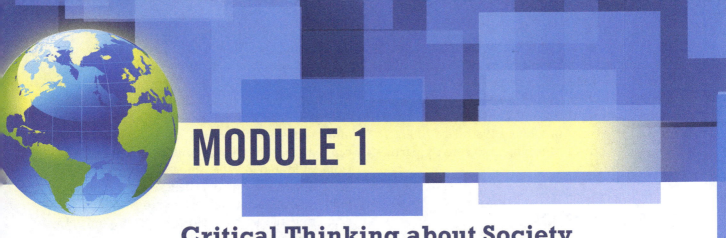

MODULE 1

Critical Thinking about Society

What Is Critical Thinking?

On March 31, 2009 at 2:40 a.m., Robert Daniel Webb, 42, entered an AM/PM convenience store west of Ellensburg, Washington armed with a handgun and demanded fuel for his car, store merchandise, and money from the cash register. Surveillance video (https://youtu.be/6--9f-FtDVI) from the robbery shows Webb committing the crime with his 9-year daughter by his side, telling the clerk he had recently lost his job and needed to care for his daughter.

Tim Kelly (2009) from the *Yakima Herald Republic* reported that Webb fled to California with his daughter to elude police. A friend of the suspect notified authorities. Three days later, Webb was captured in Yakima, Washington, and his daughter was released to her mother. During Webb's arraignment, the judge asked if he had been convicted previously of any crimes. Webb replied he had no prior felony convictions.

As people navigate their way through life, they often forget how their thinking and behavior impact others around them. For instance, Robert Daniel Webb (even with good intentions to provide for his family) did not consider the risk he placed on himself, his daughter, the store clerk, or the community by robbing the store. Individuals can become so consumed by their own thoughts and needs that they lose sight of how everyone is interconnected in society.

Sociology explores how individual thinking and behavior influence the social world. The social world people create then influences thinking and behavior. This is a cyclical process constructing the world in which people live. If thinking lacks critical evaluation and analysis, then the behavior or actions that follow are more likely to be unproductive or even damaging to the social world. Critical thinking is the foundation for ensuring the social world is just, caring, and sustainable for the human race.

FIGURE 1

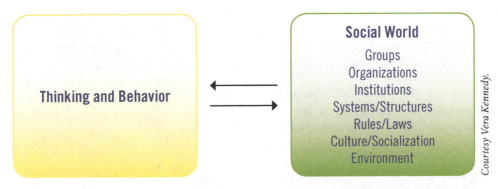

Thinking and Behavior

Social World
Groups
Organizations
Institutions
Systems/Structures
Rules/Laws
Culture/Socialization
Environment

Courtesy Vera Kennedy.

People define critical thinking in many ways. In evaluating the body of research on the subject, critical thinking is best described as a process of **constant reflection and questioning** that **challenges assumptions and context** while **exploring alternatives** (Brookfield 1986; Tice 2000). To engage in critical thinking is to actively participate in thinking.

Characteristics of Critical Thinking

The act of **reflection and questioning** is to engage in thinking about your thoughts and the thoughts of others or, simply stated, to "think about thinking." Though this concept sounds easy to perform, its practice is difficult to carry out without conscious effort. People think all the time, every day, but to identify, analyze, and evaluate each thought is difficult, especially when critical thinking identifies fallacious or unsubstantiated thoughts.

Finding flaws in one's thinking can feel threatening. People experience **cognitive dissonance** when their perceptions are challenged. Cognitive dissonance refers to the mental discomfort or anxiety a person feels when confronted with new values, beliefs, ideas, or information that is contrary to their own. Cognitive dissonance affects people differently—some embrace new ideas and ways of thinking while others retreat, deny new perspectives, and retain pre-existing notions (Corey 1991). People who respond to the cognitive dissonance by asking questions about why they might be experiencing that anxiety undergo internal cognitive changes building intellectual capacity (Brookfield 1986; Tice 2000). Confronting cognitive dissonance builds the mind and opens new pathways in thinking, even when a conclusion is reached that results in retaining the original idea or perspective.

When people make a conscious effort to reflect and question their own thinking, they invite their mind to consider the influence of assumptions and context. Because **assumptions** are made using personal beliefs or a hypothetical guess, they may be based on bias, stereotypes, judgments, and past experiences. How people perceive the world and their place in it is often derived from what they believe to be true, and perception does not always match with reality. An individual's perception is not always substantiated or constructed from valid and reliable information or sources. For example, many people believe those receiving public assistance or welfare do not work and are exploiting the system. However, approximately 67% of families living below the poverty line had at least one family member working, with 25% of them having at least one member working full-time year round (U.S. Bureau of the Census 2014). Challenging assumptions like this requires exposing and examining personal and social truths using complete and accurate information.

Our perceptions of ourselves and others and our social and physical environment are influenced by and rooted in various contexts. The setting or situation builds the **context** of thought and influences our behavior. Yelling and screaming in a place of worship is significantly different than yelling and screaming at a sporting event. Each context has built-in acceptable and unacceptable behaviors. Within each environment, context is constructed in forming normative responses and actions. Challenging context requires considering the necessity and appropriateness of prescribed boundaries and norms (i.e., formal and informal social rules) while recognizing cultural and social differences in environments or settings.

The critical thinking process relies on constant reflection and questioning for developing alternatives to challenge assumptions and context. The consideration of **alternatives** leads people to challenge perspectives (singular points of view) and paradigms (patterns of viewpoints). Thinking about alternatives generates options or choices for framing or understanding oneself and the social world. Exploring alternatives helps eliminate narrow-minded thinking and allows the mind to gather new information and formulate innovative, original, or authentic ideas.

TABLE 1

Characteristics of Critical Thinking	Real World Application
1. Reflect and Question	"Think about thinking" requires identification, analysis, and evaluation of thought
2. Challenge Assumptions	To challenge assumptions, one must identify, analyze, and evaluate: • Beliefs • Truths • Facts • Sources
3. Consider Context	To consider context, one must identify, analyze, and evaluate: • Setting • Situation • Environment • Boundaries • Norms • Cultural and social differences
4. Explore Alternatives	To explore alternatives, one must identify, analyze, evaluate: • Perspectives • Paradigms • Information • Options

Courtesy Vera Kennedy.

How Critical Thinking Works

People use rationality, personal experience, and emotions to think critically. These three forms of inquiry work together in the critical thinking process. At any time, one form of analysis can have a greater influence on critical thinking than others.

Rationality is based on logic and reasoning. Therefore, rationality is not always grounded in factual data, but from an evaluation of information based on a person's experience, knowledge, and thinking patterns. Because rationality is highly influenced by pre-existing information, social and cultural upbringing often affects a person's perceptions and assumptions that form his or her ideas.

Practicing the art of critical thinking requires an internal evaluation of a person's reasoning or logic. Part of being a rational thinker is to not simply question information and the thinking of others, but questioning and reflecting personal thought processes, including an examination or inquiry of one's own logic and rationale in decision-making.

When people apply logic or reasoning skills, they have a tendency to make decisions using probability or possibility. Using past experiences or knowledge to predict the future or outcome is the application of probability otherwise known as **inductive reasoning**. Inductive reasoning is effective when sound predictions can be made with minimal error. For example, people generally predict the day will produce daylight and the night will produce moonlight.

Activities that require the application of protocols, rules, or regulations without independent judgment use **deductive reasoning**. Deductive reasoning leaves no room for predictions, alterations, or creativity. Because rules are prescribed, decisions are made within boundaries. Balancing a checkbook requires adherence to the rules of mathematics. Driving a car requires adherence to the protocols of physics as well as the rules and regulations of the law.

This does not mean rationality relies solely on probability or a prescribed set of rules. People also make decisions using empirical and ideological reasoning. **Empirical reasoning** tests a hypothesis using observable information. The **scientific method** used in research incorporates empirical reasoning in the collection and analysis of data. The scientific method is a process people follow to test their questions and explore perspectives, but there are no set rules associated with what might be observed or discovered. Because this form of reasoning tests premises using observational data, it aligns with inductive reasoning.

Ideological reasoning is founded on a person's core values, beliefs, and principles. People adhere to faith in their ideology as the rule in decision-making. All rules are socially constructed whether they are based facts (social rules) or personal truths (individual rules). In reasoning, people sometimes choose to make decisions based on either social or personal rules. For example, the decision to pick a nose in public is a social rule while the decision to undergo cosmetic surgery for aesthetic purposes is a personal rule. The use of incorporating value judgments in decision-making aligns this form of rationality to deductive reasoning.

Poor or invalid reasoning must be examined when applying and evaluating rationality. These flaws in reasoning are called **fallacies**. Linked to assumptions, fallacies may appear correct but are derived from inaccurate or incomplete information. Even when analyzing empirical data, results can be misinterpreted. Contrary to the popular saying "data speak for themselves," data never speak for themselves and require interpretation. For example, in June 2011, a number of news sources reported the findings from a study linking the consumption of diet soda to weight gain and increased sugar levels in the blood stream (Fowler, Williams, and Hazuda 2015). While the research revealed a connection between artificial sugars and sweeteners in diet soda to size of waistlines and blood sugar levels, some news outlets misinterpreted the results of the study

FIGURE 2

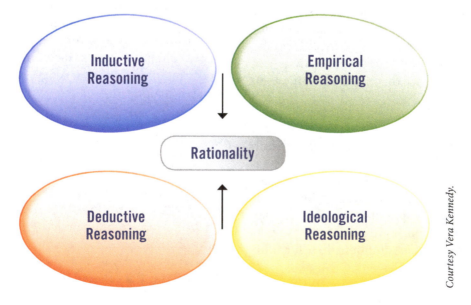

Courtesy Vera Kennedy.

(see https://youtu.be/Io2nWfR_Keo). It is not the consumption of diet soda but consumption of artificial sugars and sweeteners that is believed to interfere with brain functioning sending signals to the body to store more calories and evaluate fasting glucose levels (UT Health Science Center San Antonio 2011). The correlation between drinking diet soda, an increased waistline, and increased blood sugar levels were not interpreted correctly or presented with the complete context to the public by some news sources, resulting in the dissemination of a fallacy that diet soda, and not the artificial sugars and sweeteners in the diet soda, was responsible for weight gain and increased sugar levels in the bloodstream.

Cognitive development is the progression of thinking ability over time. People develop cognition through socialization or learning from others. The highest form of cognitive development requires critical thinking.

A person's **experience** influences development, knowledge, and thinking. The ability to reason and think logically is associated with a person's experience. An appropriate decision or solution may appear logical and founded on reasoning, but its strength and accuracy is dependent on the quality of the associated experience (including knowledge about the issue). A person's reasoning or problem-solving skills are only as strong as his or her experience with an issue, topic, or situation.

The initial stages of development begin at birth. Infants' first experiences develop from their interactions within the social world. From birth, infants learn to associate their place in the world by thinking about fulfilling their primary needs

Sociological Application 1.1

How do you use logic or reasoning in making decisions?

Imagine you are responding to call for action in your community. The mayor has asked citizens of your town to adopt a social problem (e.g., bullying, domestic violence, gay rights, climate change, human trafficking, hunger, identity theft, poverty, voting rights restrictions, etc.) and work with local community-based organizations to improve or change the condition.

Consider the following:

1. What community social problem will you address?
2. What factors affect your decision in choosing which social problem to adopt?
3. What role do you see yourself taking in this call for action?
4. How will you initiate your involvement in the call to action? Identify the specific steps you will complete to get involved.

After thinking about and documenting your responses, evaluate how you used rationality in your decision-making.

1. Did you follow any specific rules (e.g., religious beliefs, legality, etc.) in making decisions? Give details.
2. Did you consider various options or probable results in making decisions? Provide examples.
3. How did you evaluate the context of each question about your involvement? What information did you use to guide your decision?
4. Which decisions would you categorize as inductive or empirical? Explain.
5. Which decisions would you categorize as deductive or ideological? Explain.

(i.e., food, water, safety, etc.). How needs are fulfilled by others influences an infant's identity and sense of self, initiating ego development (Erikson 1950; Loevinger and Wessler 1970). The **ego** is the perception of self in comparison to others.

As children continue to grow, interactions with others further influence the development of a person's social self. As people develop, they learn to recognize the needs of others and balance personal needs with social needs (Mead 1934). The **social self** is the acknowledgment and awareness of others in the social world.

When individuals fail to consider the needs of others and focus on fulfilling their personal needs, they formulate egocentric thinking. **Egocentrism** is a narrow-minded, self-serving perspective that lends itself to egotism, prejudice, self-justification, and self-deception (Paul and Elder 2005a). This perspective re-enforces self-importance and the concept that "the world revolves around me."

When thinking is egotistical, negative ideas or **prejudice** develop towards others who think and behave in ways that do not benefit or promote a person's own self-interest. Because egocentric thinking focuses on fulfillment of personal needs, this practice lends itself to self-justification and self-deception. People primarily concerned about themselves **justify** their thinking with evidence that supports their ideas and thoughts and discredits those that have no personal benefit or gain. This practice is accompanied by **deception** or denial of truth or facts to preserve the ego.

Egocentric thinking values self over others. Combating egocentric thinking requires critical analysis of doing what is right or **ethical** for the well-being of everyone regardless of selfish desires. Ethical reasoning requires deliberate practice and fair-minded concern for others.

Egocentric thinking is culturally and socially embedded. A person learns how to perceive and understand the world from others. Society influences the information and messages individuals receive including values, beliefs, norms, language (including symbolic language), and material goods. These cultural elements are taught and passed down to generations, providing instruction on how to live.

Culture is taken for granted, and people assume many aspects of culture are natural or normal. The cultural explanations individuals receive from family, friends, school, work, and media justify one's own culture as the standard for how to live. As a result, people tend to think their culture is true, right, and moral which re-enforces ethnocentric thinking (Kottak and Kozaitis 2012).

Sociological Application 1.2

Why are people dishonest?

RSA Animate produced a short video discussing the circumstances in which people lie, cheat, or deceive others. View the film then answer the questions below.

The Truth about Dishonesty
http://youtu.be/XBmJay_qdNc

1. How do people self-justify and self-deceive dishonest behavior?

2. How did egocentric thinking (i.e., egotism, prejudice, self-justification, and self-deception) influence the financial crisis in the United States?

3. Do people need to be dishonest to achieve success or get ahead in life? What are the personal and social consequences of dishonesty?

Ethnocentrism is the practice of using personal cultural standards to judge others. People defend ethnocentric thinking and behavior in the same manner as egocentrism—through self-justification and self-deception. Denial is the most common defense for ethnocentric thinking. To reject how values, beliefs, norms, language (including symbolic language), and material goods influence personal perceptions and understanding of the world is to reject the influence people have on each other. However, people cannot make decisions without knowledge developed from a source. Each source influences the way people think and see things, resulting in the decisions individuals make and behaviors they portray.

The use of culture as a marker for navigating life stems from social groups. Because social development originates from family, friends, school, work, and media, people develop a narrow-minded view based on the cultural standards set by the social group(s) to which they belong. Not only do people develop self-centered viewpoints about the world, they also acquire group-centered perspectives. **Sociocentrism** is the practice of using social group standards to judge others. Similar to ethnocentrism where a person's culture is viewed as superior to others, sociocentrism centers on the superiority of the group's standards as true, right, and moral.

We can apply both an ethnocentric and sociocentric perspective to the issue of infanticide. Infanticide or infant homicide—the intentional killing of children under the age of 12 months—has been practiced everywhere in the world throughout history. Some groups adopted the practice to control births and others for sacrificial rituals. Cases of infanticide have a variety of explanations, including religious, economic, psychological, sex selection, and population control. Modern cases of infanticide have been to prevent the birth of an unwanted child (e.g., China's "one-child policy") or selective sex (e.g., India, China, and Nepal prefer sons to carry on the family name and collect inheritance).

An evaluation of infanticide from a truly objective perspective is difficult. Personal and social bias influences how this practice is interpreted and judged. For example, how someone defines the point at which life begins—is it at conception, after three months gestation, when there's a heartbeat, or at birth?—and the value of life itself is developed from cultural upbringing and re-enforced by the social group. If you were raised in a community where infanticide is valued as true, right, and moral, then you would likely judge the practice positively. If you were raised in a community where infanticide is devalued, then you would be likely to judge the practice negatively. Objectivity is limited to the cultural and social experiences influenced and the context in which one is raised.

The practice of infanticide judged positively or negatively from a personal perspective (resulting from ethnocentric and sociocentric influences) does not mean the judgment is true, right, and moral for all people or in all situations. Issues like this raise contention between people and groups because of narrow-minded thinking and a lack of understanding about different ways of life.

Emotions cue internal thought processes and play a pivotal role in critical thinking. When a person feels happy, positive thoughts are invoked. When a person feels sad, negative thoughts follow. Other emotions work the same way. Fear and anxiety can lead to defensiveness, causing one to retreat or flee. Trust can lead to acceptance causing one to open up and engage with others. Understanding our personal (internal) and social (external) emotions help us evaluate our thoughts and the resulting behaviors. Feelings play a significant role in how people draw conclusions and take action or not.

People believe emotions deter a person's ability to be logical or think rationally. However, emotions enhance intuition and play an integral role in good judgment and decision-making. Emotions allow for empathy, understanding of others, and trigger cognitive dissonance that challenge a person's thinking.

What influences your ethical decisions?

Pre-test. Imagine you have the opportunity to help someone tackling adversity in your community. Without knowing any specific details about the individual's demographic composition or personal experiences, which would you choose to help if only the following descriptions were provided?

1. Homeless
2. Prostitute
3. Psychiatric patient
4. Drug addict

Now, explain how you decided whom to help. What logic or reasoning did you use make your decision? Did any personal experiences influence your choice? How did your emotions or feelings about any of these individuals affect your choice?

Post-test. Let's suppose we just received additional information about the individuals listed above. With these new descriptors, whom would you choose to help?

1. Homeless veteran
2. Male teen prostitute
3. Child psychiatric patient
4. Prescription drug addict

Again, how did you decide whom to help. What logic or reasoning did you use to make your decision? Did any personal experiences influence your choice? How did your emotions or feelings about any of these individuals affect your choice?

Analysis. Now, review your decision-making process in the Pre-test and Post-test above.

1. Did you change your mind about who to help in the Post-test as compared to the Pre-test? Explain why you either changed your mind or not.
2. What forms of inquiry influenced your decisions in both tests: rationality, personal experience, and emotions? Rank the effect of each from most influential to least.
3. What was your true motivation for choosing the person you selected? Did you choose to help someone because the person truly needed your assistance? Did you choose someone to make yourself feel good? Did you choose someone because you could relate to that person or had a past experience with someone like them? Did you choose someone because you felt sorry or compassion for the person?
4. What cultural influences (i.e., values, beliefs, norms, language, and material goods) and social group influences (i.e., family, community, nation, and media) affected your choices?
5. In making your decision about whom to help, were your choices based on selflessness or self-interest?
6. What egocentric tendencies influenced your choices (i.e., egotism, prejudice, self-justification, and/or self-deception)?
7. What do your responses show you about how you make ethical decisions?

Social groups play a primary role in patterns of action and feelings. The excitement or hostility of a crowd can influence the emotions of everyone sharing an experience or event. For example, spectators at a sporting event create an emotional atmosphere for each other and the athletes playing the game. You are more likely to cheer or cheer more loudly when you are at the ballpark, arena, and/or stadium than if you are watching the game at home by yourself.

Because emotions play a pivotal role in critical thinking, some people play on emotions to garner support or interest. Emotions may be used to regulate discourse, condition subjectivity, or script events (Schwalbe, Godwin, Holden, Schrock, Thompson, and Wolkomir 2000). Emotion management is used by advertisers and the media to develop an audience and sell products. Politicians also use emotion-laden language to express their position on issues to garner support and deter the opposition.

During major holidays or national events, the government and media work together to frame sentiments and feelings through emotion management. Since 2001, the United States government has instituted a national day to honor and commemorate the lives lost in the terrorist attacks on September 11 at the World Trade Center site and Pentagon. Each year a national event is staged to remember those who died, influencing sentiments of sadness, cohesiveness, pride, nationalism, and patriotism. The annual event not only plays a role in helping the nation overcome the devastation of the attacks, but it also invigorates support for the country and the fight against terrorism.

The Strength of Critical Thinking

Everyone faces challenges about either life, career, finances, or affairs of the heart, and it is one's ability to analyze, evaluate, and solve problems that leads to well-informed decisions. Critical

Sociological Application 1.4

Are your beliefs based on peresonal truths or facts?

Personal experience and the time period in which we live influence our knowledge base used in thinking. Morgan Spurlock hosted a television series called *30 Days*, exploring how people are able to change their perceptions and thinking simply by exposing themselves to new people and cultural experiences. You can read a summation of the episode entitled "Muslims and America" at: http://www.realityshack.com/archives/1228. The full episode is available online for rent or purchase.

After reading about the experiences of Dave Stacey in the 30 Days episode "Muslims and America," describe your perceptions about Christians and Muslims and then evaluate your thinking using the **Characteristics of Critical Thinking** in Table 1.

1. What do you know to be true about Christians?

2. What do you know to be true about Muslims?

3. How do you know these things to be true? Did you base your responses on logic, personal experience, or emotions? Explain.

4. Are there gaps in your critical thinking process? Did you challenge assumptions, consider context, explore alternatives, and question and reflect?

5. What can you do to improve your critical thinking skills? How will you practice these new skills?

thinking is the foundation of good decision-making. By effectively analyzing, evaluating, and problem-solving, one is using **strategic thinking** directly derived from the critical thinking process needed for solving complex issues.

Critical strategic thinking requires foresight and knowledge and involves challenging conventional thought using valid and reliable sources, which establishes **credibility** of thought. A critical thinker views personal and social issues from multiple perspectives (both small- and large-scale) and looks ahead to anticipate possible outcomes or obstacles. Additionally, a good thinker questions whether a source is accurate, trustworthy, and legitimate. The possibility of bias (subjectivity) and hidden agendas is reviewed in their examination of sources.

Aside from the personal gains associated in being a critical thinker, there are social strengths and benefits as well. Critical thinkers are consciously aware of their thinking and the thoughts of others. Using critical thinking to solve complex issues provides insight into other people and plays a strong role in identifying ways people might work together in making good choices and decisions. So, not only does critical thinking reenforce analytical thought, but it also facilitates **teamwork** resulting from the insights gained by "thinking about thinking."

Reflecting on the thinking of others gives insight into the diversity of life among people. Critical thinking develops understanding about others and fuels **empathy**. The exchange of thoughts, experiences, and ideas while contemplating, creates a context or environment for helping people put themselves in the "shoes of others" and

Sociological Application 1.5

What is your EQ?

Several online tests can be taken to assess one's emotional intelligence or capacity for empathy with others. Take the Empathy Quotient (EQ) Test at http://www.guardian.co.uk/life/table/0,,937442,00.html.

How did you score? Do you feel your results accurately reflect your tendency and capacity for empathy?

What your score means

On average, most women score about 47 and most men about 42. Most people with Asperger Syndrome or high-functioning autism score about 20.

0–32 = You have a lower than average ability for understanding how other people feel and responding appropriately.

33–52 = You have an average ability for understanding how other people feel and responding appropriately. You know how to treat people with care and sensitivity.

53–63 = You have an above average ability for understanding how other people feel and responding appropriately. You know how to treat people with care and sensitivity.

64–80 = You have a very high ability for understanding how other people feel and responding appropriately. You know how to treat people with care and sensitivity.

If you found this interesting and insightful, you might consider taking another online assessment, such as http://www.empathystyles.com/findoutyourstyles.php, http://www.realtestsonline.com/personality-tests/empathy-test.cfm, or http://www.gotoquiz.com/the_empathy_test.

understand associated references from the perspective of others.

The Empathy Quotient (EQ) Test (several interesting online empathy quizzes are available; this one is based on this website: http://www.guardian.co.uk/life/table/0,,937442,00.html. Other recommended assessments in rank order include: http://www.empathystyles.com/findoutyourstyles.php, http://www.realtestsonline.com/personality-tests/empathy-test.cfm, and http://www.gotoquiz.com/the_empathy_test).

The Empathy Quotient is intended to measure how easily you pick up on other people's feelings and how strongly you are affected by other people's feelings.

Core Critical Thinking Skills

On the road to becoming an effective critical thinker, there are **six core skills** to develop. These skills include interpretation, analysis, inference, evaluation, explanation, and self-regulation (American Philosophical Association 1990). Each skill assists in implementing the characteristics of critical thinking. These skills provide the tools needed to analyze and evaluate evidence, concepts, methods, criteria, and context (American Philosophical Association 1990). People must train their minds and deliberately practice the core skills to become effective critical thinkers.

The ability to **interpret** means one is able to process, understand, and frame meaning about observations (including data). Interpretation is the first level of deciphering and sorting information and interactions in the critical thinking process. If observations are misinterpreted or not clearly understood, then thinking may become burdened with assumptions and fallacies.

Analysis requires a systematic or methodological process to dissect observations. This skill plays a key role in the ability to interpret and explain information and interactions. Strong analytical skills are developed by training the mind to examine, study, and scrutinize observations or data.

An **inference** is an intellectual act leading to a conclusion about whether something is true or not (Paul and Elder 2005b). The mind makes an interpretation based on what is observed. Inferences can be accurate or inaccurate, logical or illogical, or justified or unjustified (Paul and Elder 2005b). Humans have a tendency to use beliefs as assumptions and then make inferences based on those assumptions.

You can increase awareness about your own inferences and assumptions by remembering others make inferences and assumptions, too. Curiosity about the origin of data, reasoning, and concerns helps develop higher levels of inquiry foster higher-level data (Kortens n.d.). Sharing assumptions and revealing data, reasoning, and concerns with others opens the

FIGURE 3

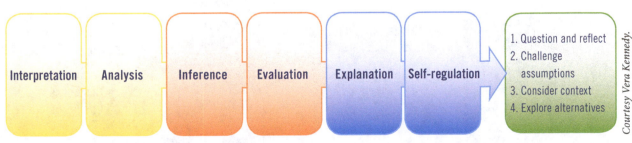

Interpretation | Analysis | Inference | Evaluation | Explanation | Self-regulation

1. Question and reflect
2. Challenge assumptions
3. Consider context
4. Explore alternatives

Courtesy Vera Kennedy.

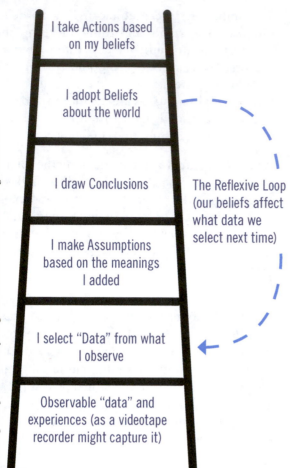

I take Actions based on my beliefs

I adopt Beliefs about the world

I draw Conclusions

The Reflexive Loop (our beliefs affect what data we select next time)

I make Assumptions based on the meanings I added

I select "Data" from what I observe

Observable "data" and experiences (as a videotape recorder might capture it)

mind and prevents misinterpretations and misunderstandings. Be careful how you "go up the ladder of inference."

Evaluation is a skill used to assess observations or data. Appraisals must investigate the origin or source of information for accuracy, relevance, validity, and truthfulness. An evaluation must also consider both or multiple perspectives regardless of position (i.e., pro or con).

Sharing results of critical analysis requires the ability to explain thinking. **Explanation** helps others understand reasoning and justification behind thinking and actions. Critical thinking is meaningless without being able to clarify statements or conclusions drawn from observations or data.

The most difficult skill to master is **self-regulation**. The ability to regulate personal viewpoints and bias is crucial to applying critical thinking from an objective perspective. Freud (1953–1966) referred to this skill as the *Superego* or consciousness, which helps balance and manages the *Id* (self-fulfillment including the need to validate thinking without concern for others) with the *Ego* (social values and norms or the needs of others). Self-regulation is literally "thinking about **one's own** thinking."

FIGURE 4

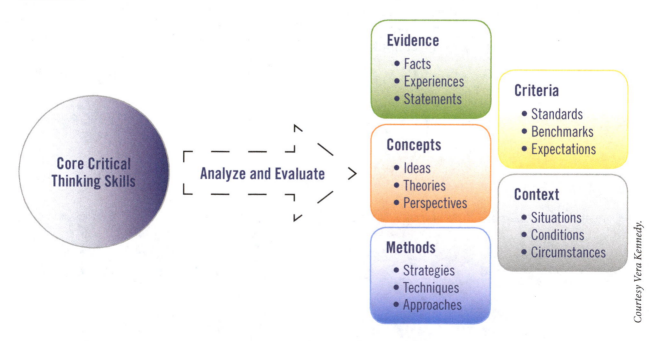

Courtesy Vera Kennedy.

Ethical Reasoning

Ethics are a set of concepts and principles that guide behavior. Ethical behavior is doing what is right, just, and honorable. Ethical people use reason and think critically to evaluation information to make decisions about various issues. Ethical decisions require an analysis of reasoning and evaluation of thinking.

Society and culture nurture pre-disposed behavior and ethics through positive and negative re-enforcement. Humans have a propensity to focus on the needs of self over others (Paul and Elder 2005a). Few people value others as much as they value self. Individuals must become proficient at assessing reasoning to develop empathy and make ethical decisions.

To guide ethical behavior, society has established universal ideologies that direct reasoning away from cultural and religious bias or judgments. As conscious beings, people are capable of understanding helping or hurting behavior. Universal ideologies evaluate ethical behavior as either helpful or harmful actions towards others (Paul and Elder 2005a). These principles converge across cultures and groups and focus on whether human behavior contributes to or damages the quality of life of another.

Sociological Application 1.6

What are human rights?

The Universal Declaration of Human Rights is a global statement of the inherent dignity and equality of all human beings. The manuscript (http://www.un.org/en/documents/udhr/) was developed by the United Nations and adopted on December 10, 1948. The content expresses the economic, social, cultural, political, and civil rights of all people throughout the world (video: http://www.youthforhumanrights.org/).

The U.S. Constitution established the government of America and laws pertaining to citizen rights. The document was signed by Constitutional Convention delegates on September 17, 1787. The articles were amended in 1791 to include the Bill of Rights (http://www.archives.gov/exhibits/charters/constitution_transcript.html) guaranteeing citizens' individual protections under the law (e.g., freedom of speech, assembly, right to bear arms, etc.).

Compare the Articles in the Universal Declaration of Human Rights (UDHR) and the U.S. Bill of Rights.

1. What rights are guaranteed in both documents? What protections do they imply?

2. What rights do you think are missing from the UDHR?

3. What rights do you think are missing from the Bill of Rights?

4. If we define a "right" as a power or privilege one is justly entitled to, list which "rights" you have been granted and denied throughout your life.

5. Reflecting on the list you created, explain how and by what codes have you and the groups you identify with been oppressed (harmed), oppressed others, or enjoyed the privileges individual or communal "rights" provide.

6. The function of the UDHR is to serve as an ethical code to entitle all human beings equal dignity and justice. Choose the Articles from the UDHR that define rights you feel most inspire or demand protection.

Many professional groups have ethical codes of conduct (i.e., physicians, judges, fundraisers, law enforcement officers, social workers, school personnel, etc.). Codes of conduct go beyond the written law and encompass general rules about lying, cheating, bribery, conflicts of interest, discrimination, and harassment. These codes not only ensure ethical behavior among groups and organizations, but they also set an example and establish a standard for ethical behavior for the community at large.

Researchers also maintain ethical guidelines to ensure the protection of study participants, transparency of research, and credibility of findings. The Office of Human Research Protections in the U.S. Department of Health and Human Services (http://www.hhs.gov/ohrp/index.html) provides regulatory oversight on biomedical and social behavioral research. To ensure the protection of study participants, researchers must obtain informed consent and maintain anonymity or confidentiality. This protection shields subjects from having personal, identifiable data released to the public. Additionally, researchers must be open, honest, and truthful about research objectives, including use and dissemination of data. The function and purpose of the research study must be clearly noted and communicated to potential participants to show transparency. Lastly, researchers are prohibited from plagiarizing, falsifying results, or misrepresenting participant responses or their own work to demonstrate the credibility of the study and researcher(s).

People are responsible for familiarizing themselves and following ethical behavior. Whether actions are intentional or unintentional, there are consequences for unethical behavior, including fines, disciplinary or corrective action (e.g., suspension) set by an organization, or legal action. It is important to establish ethical guidelines to avoid unethical behavior. The overarching rule is "no harm to others." This principle ensures a general framework for behavior that treats others with respect (by avoiding inappropriate or offensive remarks), treats everyone fairly, and focuses on ethical resolutions in the face of conflict.

Critical Service Learning Pedagogy

One of the central themes surrounding critical thinking is its function in decision-making. A critical thinker creates a foundation for effectively solving personal and social problems by making thoughtful, just decisions. Critical thinking plays a significant role in empowering individuals and communities into agents of change to improve the social conditions in which people live.

Everyone participates in communities, but not everyone lives to his or her full potential and takes his or her place in transforming the systems of power that create inequality and violate human rights. Living in and serving a community goes beyond social responsibility. Everyone has an ethical obligation to actively engage in communities for social justice. "Social justice includes a vision of society that is equitable [i.e., fair] and all members are physically and psychologically safe and secure" (Bell, Adams, and Griffin 2007). People like to believe if they are not part of the problem then they have no responsibility in creating or becoming part of the solution. However, the sociological perspective informs us that one person's problem eventually becomes everyone's problem. Social problems touch communities whether through living conditions, taxation, fees, civil liberties, policies, or laws. The consequences of personal issues affect everyone and often result in unjust and oppressive social structures that further the social inequality by either ignoring, relocating, or locking up the problem rather than solving it.

Instead of breeding structures of inequality, critical service pedagogy suggests community members (including students and faculty) re-imagine their roles in solving social problems by deconstructing systems of power through service to their communities. It is not enough to feed the hungry, but more important to ask the question why people are hungry and investigate how the problem is being sustained in the broader social context. Critical thinking raises questions about the roots of social inequality and generates social awareness by examining the political and economic decisions that make hunger possible (Mitchell 2008). Critical service is not about "doing service"; instead, it's about reflecting on the service and the assumptions and stereotypes of the individuals and communities being served. The goal of critical service is community transformation through social change. In this approach, service to the community should not be directed at volunteerism that may cultivate negative feelings or stereotypes about the people being served (re-enforces oppression) or to re-enforce egocentric tendencies to feel good by serving those "less fortunate" (re-enforces privilege).

To actively participate in critical service, people must foster critical consciousness, combining action and reflection. Each person should, on some personal level, connect with the lives of those with whom they serve and contemplate how personal and institutional contributions or measures might lead to social change (Marullo 1999; Rice and Pollack 2000). Each person must question and investigate the root causes of social problems, including systematic and institutionalized oppression, and work in partnership with the community to take the actions necessary to alter them those social arrangements. Everyone plays a role in the critical service process, contributing their skills and knowledge to making large-scale changes in the community.

Critical service means analyzing a social issue and then proposing and implementing a change with others with vested interest or shared concern. By learning the critical service approach, people become empowered and see they are capable of acting together, fostering awareness, and creating social change (Forbes, Garber, Kensinger, and Slagter 1999). Everyone is a teacher and everyone is a learner. This approach brings together community knowledge, builds authentic

FIGURE 5

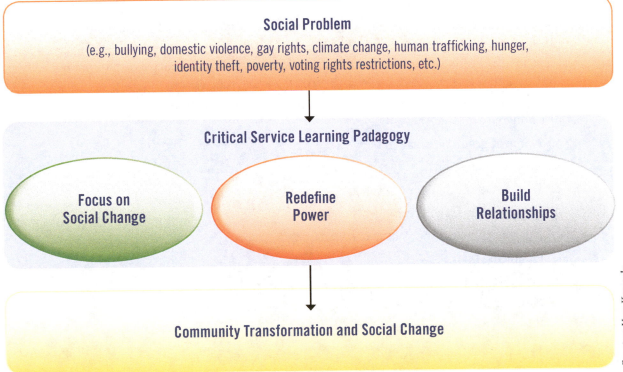

Courtesy Vera Kennedy.

What will be your legacy?

People often wait until they approach retirement to begin thinking about their legacy. At that time, it is too late. Our legacy begins at adulthood, when we leave behind parental restrictions and begin to make our way into the world. It is from our first steps of independence that we begin to leave a footprint of how we will be remembered by others. The people we come into contact with along with our accomplishments and failures become the memories we instill. What you do in this world and how you treat others will be the legacy you leave behind.

In Sociological Application 1.1, you were asked to respond to call for action in your community. The mayor asked citizens of your town to adopt a social problem (e.g., bullying, domestic violence, gay rights, climate change, human trafficking, hunger, identity theft, poverty, voting rights restrictions, etc.) and work with local community based organizations to improve or change the condition. Reflect back on the social issue you selected to address and the role and steps you suggested taking to become involved.

Using the social issue identified in Sociological Application 1.1, develop a research portfolio on the topic as your initial step to developing a *Critical Service Learning Plan*:

1. Define the social problem.
   a. History of the problem
   b. Social arrangements (i.e., individuals/groups involved and their relationships)
   c. Labels depicted or associated with the problem
   d. Power structure and relationships

2. Discuss the impact of the problem on the community and society (i.e., economic, environmental, biological, psychological, and social).

3. Describe the individuals, group, or category of people directly impacted and/or oppressed by the problem (i.e., age, gender, race/ethnicity, education, income, etc.).

4. Identify any people, groups, or organizations working to solve the problem in your community and explain what they are doing.
   a. Name of group or organization
   b. Mission statement
   c. Leadership (i.e., CEO or Director)
   d. Organizational structure
   e. Number of members, volunteers, staff
   f. Operating budget
   g. Population serving
   h. Number of clients
   i. Location of service delivery

Continued

5. Interview an organizational leader working to solve the problem to learn about the history of the problem and organization from their point of view and the initiatives, services, and solutions being implemented or planned throughout the community.

   a. Ask leaders to recommend people directly impacted by the problem to interview.

6. Interview a community member directly impacted by the problem to gain personal insight about the problem and the challenges and/or obstacles faced on a daily basis.

7. Evaluate if current initiatives or solutions are working to eradicate the problem.

relationships, dispels myths about the issue or needs, and eliminates stigmatizing labels of those being served as the oppressed and those serving as the privileged. The success of critical service is dependent on the connective relationships built within the community in pursuit of shared goals through respect and trust (Mitchell 2008). Critical service is inclusive and recognizes the impact of social issues on everyone and how every person has a responsibility to create a just and caring society.

References

American Philosophical Association. 1990. *Critical Thinking: A Statement of Expert Consensus for Purposes of Educational Assessment and Instruction*. Millbrae, CA: The California Academic Press.

Adams, Maurianne, Lee Anne Bell, and Pat Griffin, Eds. 2007. *Teaching for Diversity and Social Justice*. 2nd edition. New York: Routledge.

Brookfield, Stephen D. 1991. *Developing Critical Thinkers: Challenging Adults to Explore Alternative Ways of Thinking and Acting*. San Francisco, CA: Jossey-Bass.

Corey, Gerald. 2012. *Theory and Practice of Counseling and Psychotherapy*. Pacific Grove, CA: Brooks/Cole.

Erikson, Erik H. 1950. *Childhood and Society*. New York: W.W. Norton & Company.

Fowler, Sharon P.G., Ken Williams, and Helen P. Hazuda. 2015. "Diet Soda Intake Is Associated with Long-Term Increases in Waist Circumference in a Biethnic Cohort of Older Adults: The San Antonio Longitudinal Study of Aging." *Journal of the American Geriatrics Society* 63(4):708–715.

Forbes, Kathryn, Linda Garber, Loretta Kensinger, and Janet T. Slagter. 1999. "Punishing Pedagogy: The Failings of Forced Volunteerism." *Women's Studies Quarterly* 3–4: 158:168.

Freud, Sigmund. 1953–1966. *Standard Edition of the Complete Psychological Works of Sigmund Freud*. London: Hogarth Press.

Kelly, Tim. 2009. "Bail Set in Robbery Case." *Yakima Herald Republic*, April 8, p. Main/Home Front.

Kortens, Tony. n.d. The Ladder of Inference. *Envision International*.

Kottak, Conrad P. and Kathryn A. Kozaitis. 2012. *On Being Different: Diversity and Multiculturalism in the North American Mainstream*. 4th ed. New York: McGraw-Hill Companies, Inc.

Loevinger, Jane and Ruth Wessler. 1970. *Measuring Ego Development*. San Francisco, CA: Jossey-Bass.

Marullo, Sam. 1999. "Sociology's Essential Role: Promoting Critical Analysis in Service-Learning." Pp. 11–27 in *Cultivating the Sociological Imagination: Concepts and Models for Service-Learning in Sociology*, edited by J. Ostrow, G. Hesser, and S. Enos. Washington, DC: American Association of Higher Education.

Mead, George Herbert. 1934. *Mind, Self and Society*. Chicago, IL: University of Chicago Press.

Mitchell, Tania D. 2008. "Traditional vs. Critical Service-Learning: Engaging the Literature to Differentiate Two Models." *Michigan Journal of Community Service Learning* 14(2):55–65.

Paul, Richard and Linda Elder. 2005a. *The Miniature Guide to Understanding the Foundations of Ethical Reasoning*. Tomales, CA: Foundation for Critical Thinking.

Paul, Richard and Linda Elder. 2005b. "Critical Thinking: Distinguishing between Inferences and Assumptions." *Critical Thinking: Tools for Taking Charge of Your Learning and Your Life*. Upper Saddle River, NJ: Prentice Hall.

Rice, Kathleen and Seth Pollack. 2000. 'Developing a Critical Pedagogy of Service Learning: Preparing Self-Reflection, Culturally Aware, and Response Community Participants." Pp. 115–134 in *Integrating Service Learning and Multicultural Education in Colleges and Universities*, edited by C. O'Grady. Mahwah, NJ: Lawrence Erlbaum Associates.

Schwalbe, Michael, Sandra Godwin, Daphne Holden, Douglas Schrock, Shealy Thompson, and Michele Wolkomir. 2000. "Generic Processes in the Reproduction of Inequality: An Interactionist Analysis." *Social Forces* 79(2):419–452.

Tice, Elizabeth T. 2000. "What is Critical Thinking?" *Journal of Excellence in Higher Education*. Phoenix, AZ: University of Phoenix.

U.S. Bureau of the Census. 2014. *Current Population Survey, 2013 and 2014 Annual Social and Economic Supplement*. Washington, DC: U.S. Government Printing Office.

UT Health Science Center San Antonio. 2011. "Related Studies Point to the Illusion of the Artificial." San Antonio, TX: The University of Texas Health Science Center at San Antonio.

Do you know the terms?

Using the list provided below, create a personal dictionary of key terms and concepts presented in this module. Include the term, phonetic spelling (if needed), and definition in your own words. Next, provide a real world example of the term or concept based on your previous knowledge or new information you learned in this module to help re-enforce learning.

Alternative	Ideological reasoning
Analysis	Inductive reasoning
Assumption	Inference
Cognitive dissonance	Interpret
Context	Prejudice
Credibility	Questioning
Deductive reasoning	Rationality
Ego	Reflection
Egocentrism	Scientific method
Emotions	Self-deception
Empathy	Self-justification
Empirical reasoning	Self-regulation
Ethical reasoning	Six core critical thinking skills
Ethnocentrism	
Evaluation	Social self
Experience	Sociocentrism
Explanation	Strategic thinking
Fallacies	Teamwork

MODULE 2

Public Sociology

Sociological Analysis

For 50 years, Charles M. Schulz wrote and illustrated a comic strip about the personal problems of a young boy named Charlie Brown, his pet dog Snoopy, and his friends. Over 17,000 *Peanuts* comic strips were published weekly in 21 languages throughout 2,600 newspapers worldwide (Michaelis 2008). Numerous media adaptations based on characters from *Peanuts* have been generated through film, television, musical theater, and video games, embedding itself into popular culture and becoming the most popular and historically influential comic strip about American life. The stories Schulz presents are not unique; they reflect upon everyone's story and shine light on commonalities of the human experience. Reading about Charlie Brown (or one of his friends) illustrates how the experiences of one character with failure, frustration, anxiety, depression, etc. are both affected by, and affect, the lives of others. The strips provide readers with a glimpse of how Charlie Brown's personal problems are truly part of larger social issues.

C. Wright Mills (1959) was the first sociologist to explain the distinction between personal problems and social issues. **Personal problems**, also seen as private troubles, are framed around an individual's social perspective and life experience, whereas **social problems**, or public issues, transcend individuals and examine the social arrangement of the masses and perspectives of

Matthew Naythons/The LIFE Images Collection/Getty Images

the public as a group, network, organization, or system. For example, over 600,000 children suffer from domestic violence each year (U.S. Department of Health and Human Services 2015). Each child affected by abuse from a family member has a unique story about his or her experiences. Each case of child abuse affects the biological and psychological state of those victimized, but each case has consequences on the family unit, law enforcement, judges, physicians, mental health professionals, and school personnel to name a few. The personal troubles of one child are tied to groups, networks, organizations, and systems within society, making domestic violence a social problem as well as a personal problem.

Interventions or resolutions addressing personal problems target change within an individual; however, social problems require social solutions and approaches. **Social interventions** aim to change the social structure including the social world and thinking and behavior of individuals. Once a significant proportion of people in a society become aware of the negative or harmful consequences of personal troubles, the private matter becomes a wider public issue and is seen as a social problem to be addressed broadly by society.

For example, let's consider high school dropout rates. Today, it is not uncommon to hear news reports, school principals, and community leaders express concern about the percentage of 16- through 24-year-olds not enrolled in school and without a high school credential (either a diploma or an equivalency credential such as a General Educational Development [GED] certificate). However, this is a "modern" concern. Prior to the 1960s, dropping out of high school was predominantly viewed as an individual, or private, problem. In fact, statistics were not even kept until 1960, and, by the way, the rate has significantly dropped from 27.2% in 1960 to 6.8% in 2013 (U.S. Department of Education 2015). So, we should ask ourselves, why weren't we, as a society concerned with high school dropout rates as a "social problem" until more recently? What do you think?

To think like a sociologist, try to understand things "in context"—that is, we investigate what else is going on in a given time period to see if that might help us explain the phenomenon we are observing. If we examine the economy in the 1940s and 1950s, we will find that many employment opportunities, including well-paid union jobs in manufacturing facilities, didn't necessarily require a high school diploma. In 2006, 70% of jobs still required no college education for entry (Hudson 2008). Today, however, more employment opportunities beyond minimum wage require at least a high school degree or equivalent credential, with more and more of them requiring a college/baccalaureate degree and even an advanced degree. The U.S. Department of Labor's Bureau of Labor Statistics projects that while total employment in the U.S. economy is expected to increase by 15.6 million jobs from 2012 to 2022, jobs requiring postsecondary education (i.e., beyond high school) are projected to grow by 14.0%, while jobs requiring a master's degree are expected to grow the fastest (18.4%), and those requiring a high school diploma will experience the slowest growth (9.1%) over the 2012–22 time frame. And, while a significant number of sub-baccalaureate jobs that offer better-than-average salaries do exist for those who go through occupational or vocational education, professional or trade associations, and/or formal apprenticeship programs, today's college graduates earn 34.1% more than those with only a two-year degree or some college, 38.5% more than those with only a high school diploma, and more than twice as much as those without a high school degree (Pew Research Center 2014). Thus, financial well-being in the 21st century is more closely related to educational degree attainment than in the past and, now, high school dropout rates are considered a "social problem" that needs to be addressed. While a number of personal issues affect one's likelihood of graduating from high school, including financial challenges, employment obligations, family issues, behavioral matters, and a lack of personal or educational support (Doll, Eslami, and Walters 2013), sociologists realize that we must also

FIGURE 6

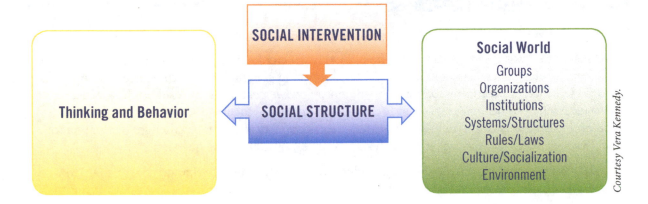

Courtesy Vera Kennedy.

examine the larger social issues, most notably our economy and future employment growth.

Social problems impact society. The structural and political arrangements of social groups often play a role in creating or sustaining social problems (e.g., poverty, unemployment, and illness) as well as resolving and eradicating the problem. Because social problems involve social arrangements, solutions go beyond any one individual.

Sociological Imagination

Learning to distinguish private, personal troubles from public, social problems requires critical thinking skills. People tend to focus on individual troubles because they stem from one's life experience and personal perspective. C. Wright Mills (1959) referred to these influences as one's history and biography. **History** reflects the time period in which a person lives and **biography** reflects the events or encounters a person experiences. Both history and biography influence individual thinking and behavior. For example, someone born in the 1920s will think and act quite differently than someone born in the 2000s. The time period each **age cohort** (i.e., people who share common experiences because they were born during the same time period) lived and the experiences they encountered shape them to view the world and their place in it differently. A person alive today who is 90 years old may or may not use a cell phone, computer, or social media in their daily activities; whereas, you might not even be able to imagine a daily routine without using at least one of these items.

The **sociological imagination**—the ability to understand how private, personal troubles are related to broader social structures—is a conceptual tool used to examine the social world beyond one's history and biography. To avoid egotistical thinking, C. Wright Mills (1959) suggested people re-examine the social world from a fresh or different perspective. Rather than looking through the lenses of one's personal history and biography, Mills recommended nurturing "new' insight by drawing on the sociological imagination. People have a tendency to examine the social world from their own place and time, and the sociological imagination suggests re-framing or considering a different vantage point to collect, process, and analyze information. Imagine sitting in the same seat every time you have dinner, attend a class, attend religious services, or go to a sporting event. The seat you sit in influences what you view during your experience and how you apply meaning to the encounter or events around you. The sociological imagination suggests you sit in a different seat to understand the people and surroundings holistically. Seeing something from one vantage point limits the information received. Viewing something from multiple perspectives creates better understanding and generates realistic, informed ideas. The sociological imagination reinforces the application of critical thinking skills in daily life to improve decision-making.

My Social Location

Our place in history and society are defined by our different dimensions of our identity (i.e., age, race, sex, gender, social class, beliefs, sexuality, ability, and geography). The categories we belong to, or are identified as belonging to, not only influence how we perceive the world but how others perceive us. Each of us occupies a place in society called our **social location**—generated by the intersection of these dimensions of our identity—that creates opportunities and challenges throughout our life. Evaluate your social location by analyzing your responses to these questions:

1. Where do you come from? Who are you? How has your identity changed over time? How do you determine or figure out your identity?

2. Which parts of your identity do you emphasize or project towards others more frequently? Which do you underplay?

3. Who are your "people"? Where or what are your "home" and "community"? How do you know this? How did you learn who you are and where home and community are? How would you find out if you don't know?

4. How many generations has your family been in the United States? What was your family's first relationship to the United States? Under what conditions did your family become part of the United States?

5. What do you know about your family's culture and history before it became part of the United States?

6. Where does your social location place you in relationship to the dominant group, minority groups, and/or immigrants in the United States? How does this affect your relationships, associations, and interactions with others?

7. Discuss specific historical events, trends, and institutions that have influenced your life. Describe your personal experiences around these events, trends, and institutions.

8. Which social dimensions of your identity (i.e., age, race, sex, gender, social class, beliefs, sexuality, ability, and geography) provide you power and privilege in society? Which aspects of your identity are affiliated with less prestige and put you at a disadvantage?

Theoretical Paradigms

In the field of sociology, six theoretical paradigms are commonly used to describe observable patterns in the social world. The theoretical paradigms provide different lenses into the social constructions of life and the relationships of people. Applying these paradigms help individuals develop a broader perspective that simulates sitting in different seats. Each paradigm provides a focus for analysis and evaluation of society to improve one's sociological imagination and avoid biased, egotistical thinking.

Two of the theoretical paradigms—Symbolic Interactionism and Exchange Theory—are microsociological perspectives. **Microsociology** refers to the study of social interactions between individuals and groups. The micro perspective observes how the thinking and behavior of individuals and groups influences the social world.

Four of the theoretical paradigms—Functionalism, Conflict Theory, Feminism, and Environmental Theory—are macrosociological perspectives. **Macrosociology** refers to the study of large-scale social arrangements (i.e., groups, organizations, networks, and systems) in the social world. The macro perspective examines how the social world influences the thinking and behavior of individuals and groups.

Exploring the microsociological and macrosociological perspectives provides insight into the relationship between thinking and behavior and the social world. Using these perspectives to investigate, research, and explore social problems provides a holistic view of the social structure surrounding an issue.

Major Theoretical Paradigms

The key to remembering and understanding the definition of each theoretical paradigm is to examine the root of the word. **Functionalism** examines function or purpose in society. Functionalism is a macrosociological perspective meaning it examines the social world (i.e., systems, organizations, networks, etc.). This paradigm focuses on how social arrangements are interrelated and the roles people play in society. We can use the human body to illustrate the Functionalist perspective. In the same way that different parts of the human body work together to create and sustain life, different aspects of society help the social world develop, sustain, and progress. For example, just as most humans have five basic senses—sight, hearing, taste, smell, and touch—human societies tend to have at least five basic social institutions—family, education, religion, economy, and government—around which society is structured.

In examining Functionalism, social arrangements result in either expected (manifest) or unexpected (latent) outcomes. An example is an act of war: governments declare war for a specific purpose and, if the anticipated goal is achieved, then the war is categorized as a **manifest function** because the result occurred the way it was imagined, expected, or designed. If on the other hand, the goal is not achieved and there are unexpected results of going to war, we would classify those outcomes as **latent functions**. For instance, some governments justify going war in order to spread democracy; sometimes a new democracy is created in the place of a former dictatorship or authoritarian regime (e.g., West Germany after WWII), but sometimes a different form of government or political instability develops, denying people in that country of life and/or civil liberties (e.g., Iraq after "Operation Iraqi Freedom").

Conflict Theory is a macrosociological paradigm examining the struggle over resources (e.g., goods, services, status, privilege, etc.) between competing groups. The application of Conflict Theory requires the identification of the people with power, those who are powerless, and the social arrangement reinforcing the power structure. An illustration of Conflict Theory is the power struggle between parents and children. Parents typically hold the legal power and financial resources to make decisions for their children. However, in examining the social relationship between parents and children, the needs of the child—food, shelter, clothing—come first, affecting the freedoms, choices, options, and needs of parents and other family members. So, parents may have legal and financial power over children, but children, at times, have social power over parents.

FIGURE 7

MICROSOCIOLOGY
(Thinking and Behavior)
Symbolic Interactionism
Exchange Theory

SOCIAL STRUCTURE

MACROSOCIOLOGY
(Social World)
Functionalism
Conflict Theory
Feminism
Environmental Theory

Courtesy Vera Kennedy.

The last major theoretical paradigm is Symbolic Interactionism. Some sociologists have shortened the reference to this perspective calling it Interactionism to focus on the root word "interaction." **Symbolic Interactionism** is a microsociological perspective examining symbols and interactions in society. This paradigm helps provides insight into how people think and behave by exploring how symbols, including words, have meaning through interaction.

A good way to remember Symbolic Interactionism is to think of the following equation: words + symbols = meaning. Applying this paradigm shows how people interpret, analyze, and evaluate the thinking and behavior of others. For example, the word "dog" and "dawg" have two very different meanings. When someone says the "dog" is at home lying on the couch, people interpret meaning as a pet and communicate visualizing an animal with fur, a tail, and whiskers. Though each person's visual image differs based on history and biography, people interpret "dog" as meaning an animal of the canine species. However, someone may have meant their "dawg" is at home lying on the couch. Because people commonly hear and use the word "dog" in their interactions, they may not be processing or thinking about the word "dawg," which is pronounced the same in the English language but has a different meaning. A "dawg" is a person referred to as a "homie" or friend. How meaning is interpreted and understood influences the context of thinking and interactions between people.

Emerging Theoretical Paradigms

This first emerging paradigm is called feminism. Even though the root word emphasizes women, this paradigm examines women and minority groups in society. **Feminism** is a macrosociological perspective examining the lives and experiences of women and minorities in the social world including the influence of these groups on society. Feminism provides a perspective into the inequality and oppression faced by women and minority groups through their lives and experiences.

The next paradigm is called exchange theory. Exchange Theory is also known as Rational Choice Theory. Regardless of which term used, the root words "exchange" means trading or swapping and "rational choice" refers to logical decisions. Both terms explain this paradigm's orientation. **Exchange Theory** is a microsociological perspective examining the thinking and behavior of people. Exchange Theory provides insight into how people make decisions by evaluating the cost versus benefit of their thinking and behavior (i.e., cost-benefit analysis). People often make decisions by assessing what the decision or action is going to cost in time, money, or resources and what is gained by the choice. Exchange Theory improves understanding about the motivation and decisions people make by examining the process of how they might have reached that decision.

The last paradigm, Environmental Theory, is often misinterpreted and confused as referencing the physical environment because of its name. **Environmental Theory** is a macrosociological perspective, also known as Postmodernism, which examines the social world (i.e., groups, organizations, systems, etc.). **Environmental Theory** focuses on how people evolve and adapt as a result of physical and social changes. For example, when people create a new law, they modify thinking and behavior to make a cultural shift. This is the case for legislative changes in recognizing gay marriage and the legalization of marijuana. This theory shines light on the surrounding environment that influences why and how people change in the social world.

Demography

In an effort to understand social problems, it is important to recognize many social problems are related. One of the challenges to solving social problems is that, usually, to solve one social problem, several others must also be addressed. This characteristic of social problems makes using demographic techniques to assess and address social problems an obvious resource. **Demography** is the study of human population statistics.

How objective are you?

Watch the short film entitled *The Middle School Moment*:
http://www.pbs.org/wgbh/pages/frontline/education/dropout-nation/middle-school-moment/

Respond, in writing, to the following questions:

1. What was your reaction or feelings about the research findings of Dr. Robert Balfanz and the prevention program adopted by Middle School 244 in the Bronx?

2. What do you agree or disagree with from the film?

3. Can you identify with or relate to Omarina Cabrera, her brother Omarlin Cabrera, or anyone else in the film?

4. What is the most important idea or concept presented in the film as it relates to critical thinking and the sociological imagination?

5. How has your history and biography influenced your reaction and viewpoint about the film and the people portrayed?

6. Describe what information presented the film would be analyzed and evaluated from a microsociological and macrosociological perspective.

7. Analyze the film using each of the six theoretical paradigms presented in Module 2. Find and explain at least one example from the film for each paradigm. For example, in applying Functionalism, the research conducted by Dr. Balfanz was conducted to identify the indicators to predict the likelihood of a student dropping out of high school. Dr. Balfanz was able to identify three indicators—student attendance, behavior, and course performance—that adequately predict risk of dropping out resulting in his research serving a manifest function.

FIGURE 8   GUIDING QUESTIONS FOR APPLYING THEORIES

Functionalism	Conflict Theory	Interactionism
What is the function or purpose of the system, institution, organization, or process represented in the social example?	Which social groups are competing over resources, which group has power, and how is power represented?	What meaning do the symbols and language represented in the example have on thinking and behavior?

Feminism	Exchange Theory	Environmental Theory
Explain the lives and experiences of women and minorities including inequality, oppression, and discrimination.	What motivates people's thinking and behavior? Describe the interest/position of the individuals represented.	How have people adapted or evolved to the social and physical context represented?

Courtesy Vera Kennedy.

Demographers, in a basic sense, are concerned with the size, distribution, structure, and change within human populations (Shyrock, Siegel, and Stockwell 1976). Initially, the discipline focused upon three main processes: fertility, mortality, and migration. Over time, the discipline has grown to include topics such as labor market patterns, poverty, and family formation patterns. Demography is inherently interdisciplinary. A variety of disciplines such as sociology, anthropology, human development and family studies, and economics rely upon demographic techniques to provide context for the issues examined within their domain. Recognizing that various disciplines must be called upon to properly address many social problems is essential to the successful resolution of these problems. Connecting to a variety of academic disciplines through demographic techniques will provide a richer and more contextually specific understanding of social problems.

Social Research

Objective vs. Subjective Analysis

Subjective data is commonly described as being open to interpretation and considered a reflection of people's perceptions, feelings, or opinions. In contrast, **objective** data is measurable, able to be observed, and based on facts. What is not always recognized is that both objective and subjective data are open to interpretation. Just as the results of subjective data analysis depend upon how information is perceived and received, results of objective data analysis may depend upon what information is included. Objective facts can be manipulated to support a variety of positions (Best 2001). For instance, if a researcher is interested in measuring poverty and, more specifically, wants to know what percentage of the United States population is poor, the result will depend on how he or she measures poverty and what he or she establishes as the cutoff or dividing line between being poor and not being poor. Still, there would be a precise formula used to derive the resulting interpretation, whether it is

biased or not. Similarly, when dealing with subjective data, a researcher might choose to focus on one comment rather than another, or he or she may choose to focus on one action instead of another. In either case, whether the researcher is dealing with objective or subjective data, having a rigorous protocol in place to conduct sociological research is critical to establishing credibility for the analysis of social problems.

Scientific Method: A Five-step Research Process

To examine social problems, a rigorous systematic protocol is necessary. This protocol involves a five-step research process, which is common to practitioners of the scientific method in both the natural and social sciences.

Step 1: The first step in the research process is to **identify the problem**. Initially, this may be a more abstract process, but, sooner rather than later, the abstract becomes concrete through the process of creating an **operational definition** of the concept. An operational concept is one that can be measured. To make a concept operational means it is possible to capture the essence of the concept with applicable measures. In this step, the researcher goes from an abstract concept to a concrete variable that can be measured. That variable, may be an independent variable or a dependent variable. An **independent variable** causes an effect or influences another variable. A **dependent variable** is the result or outcome that has been created by the effect of the independent variable. For example, a researcher may be interested in how watching television—the independent variable—impacts school performance—the dependent variable. These are general concepts that must be made operational or measurable. In establishing measures, it is important to make sure that they are valid. **Validity** refers to whether a researcher is really measuring or capturing what he or she claims to be measuring. In the example above, the researcher may decide to look at how the amount of time spent watching television impacts a student's grades. In this example, the researcher would have to find a way to measure how much television students watch. What if the researcher decided to monitor remotely when the television was on with the help of the local cable company? Do you think this be a valid measure of how much time a student spent watching television? Why or why not? Well, just because the television is on doesn't mean the student is the person watching it. It is possible no one is home or the student may be in another room or asleep while the television is on. Once it is clear the concept is measurable or able to be captured, the next step in the research process is to become an expert on the topic by reviewing the existing research.

Step 2 involves a thorough **review of the literature**. This is a critical step in the research process, which is frequently overlooked in terms of its significance. In this step, the researcher becomes an expert on the topic by thoroughly reviewing the literature. Doing so provides the basis or foundation for understanding how concepts the researcher is considering for study are connected. The models and measures others have developed will be examined during this stage of the research process. Ultimately, reviewing the literature in a thorough manner ensures the researcher will not reinvent the wheel unnecessarily; rather, the researcher will be able to recognize the gaps in the research and determine how his or her research can begin to fill the gap. Taking the time to immerse oneself in the work of others on the chosen topic can make the next step of the research process much easier.

Step 3 of the research process is to **formulate a hypothesis**, or to speculate about how two or more variables are related. When one invests the time to become an expert on a topic, developing credible explanations for how the variables are related will be less challenging. Using the example from Step 1, a researcher might hypothesize that the more television a student watches, the worse his or her grades will be. Ideally, it would be possible to prove causal relationships, but this is not always achievable. Correlations between variables are less challenging to prove. It is easy to determine whether two variables are moving at the same time. If the independent variable changes when there is a change in the dependent variable,

then a correlation is present. To determine if a causal relationship is present, proper **causal logic** must be in place, control variables must be established, and **spurious** relationships have to have been taken into consideration and then dismissed. Proper **causal logic** refers to identifying independent variables that precede the dependent variable. If the independent variable does not precede the dependent variable, then it is not possible for it to influence or effect change in the dependent variable since it did not even exist prior to the existence of the dependent variable (Neuman 2009). For instance, a former student submitted his proposed plan to study education and race. He hypothesized that a person's education level would determine his or her race. Unfortunately, this student's causal logic was not in order. Obviously, his dependent variable (i.e., a person's race) preceded the independent variable (i.e., the person's education level). A **spurious** relationship exists when two variables are statistically related and yet have no causal relation. For example, just because ice cream consumption and drownings both increase when the temperature becomes hotter does not mean that ice cream consumption causes people to drown.

Step 4: Collect and analyze the data. This begins with a **random sample** that will allow the researcher to generalize any findings. A random sample ensures every member of the population has an opportunity to participate in the study. To achieve this goal every n^{th} person or home in a particular census tract will be targeted as study subjects or potential members of the sample. Of course, if the researcher wanted to target a specific demographic group such as Type 2 diabetes patients, then a snowball or purposive/convenience sample would work best. A **convenience sample** is constructed by recruiting members of a specific population from places where they frequently spend time. For instance, flyers to recruit diabetes patients might be distributed at a diabetes support group or at a wellness center focusing on endocrinal diseases. Once the sample is selected and a protocol for collecting the data has been established and implemented, then the data can be processed and analyzed.

FIGURE 9

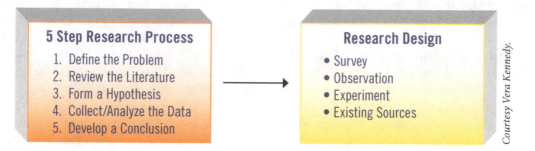

Courtesy Vera Kennedy.

Step 5: Develop conclusions. Finally, after the data is analyzed, conclusions can be drawn in the fifth and final step of the research process. In this stage of the research process, the researcher is able to determine whether support was found for the initial hypotheses. If the hypotheses are supported by the findings, the researcher's initial predictions based on the pre-existing literature are validated. If the hypotheses are not supported by the findings, the research must speculate why that is so, especially given the previous research on the topic. There is a tendency to treat a lack of support for the hypotheses as a failure, but this is a limiting perspective from which to interpret such a result. A more mindful interpretation of results that do not support the hypothesis is to recognize the new insights that may be gained from a finding that is different from that found in the prior research. A finding of non-support for a hypothesis tells us just as much about the phenomenon under study, and it may tell us even more. In this stage, it is also important to discuss any number of variables that have been controlled for or held constant to isolate the impact of the main independent variable of interest.

Research Design: Quantitative and Qualitative

In the realm of the social sciences, conflict over the value of quantitative and qualitative methodologies has raged. Quantitative methodologists and qualitative methodologists are frequently less than confident in each other's methods. In reality, both types of research have considerable challenges. Neither is perfect. The two can actually complement each other, if the practitioners

of each methodology can rise above **methodocentric** notions of that one method is superior to the other. **Quantitative** researchers rely primarily on survey research, which involves administering a questionnaire or conducting an interview in which a series of closed-ended questions are asked. Quantitative research focuses on macroanalysis, which uses **numerical data** and statistics to identify patterns in thinking and behavior. A major challenge to this type of research is convincing people to participate. Having adequate resources, such as money and people to administer the survey, is challenging as well. There are also concerns about trusting the study subjects to provide truthful and unbiased answers. In contrast, **qualitative** researchers rely on observations either as participants or non-participants. Qualitative research focuses on microanalysis, which uses **categorical data** derived from interviews, photographs, and images to understand how people think and why they behave in a particular way. In some cases, the observation period may be quite extensive, and the field operation is known as ethnography. Examples of such work include *All Our Kin* (1974) and *Hustling and Other Hard Work: Lifestyles in the Ghetto* (1978). Regardless of the length of the observation, this methodology poses some challenges. Just observing others without participating can make the subjects of the study feel self-conscious and the researcher may produce a **Hawthorne Effect**, which occurs when study participants behave differently because they are aware of being observed (Franke and Kaul 1978). Operating as a participant observer also has serious consequences. It may be more difficult to make objective observations as a participant of the group being observed. A participant observer

FIGURE 10

MICROSOCIOLOGY
(Thinking and Behavior)

Qualitative approach
- Interviews
- Participant observation
- Ethnography
- Case studies

SOCIAL STRUCTURE

MACROSOCIOLOGY
(Social World)

Quantitative approach
- Surveys
- Questionnaires
- Experiments

Courtesy Vera Kennedy.

TABLE 2

If the researcher decides to collect his or her *own data*, then he or she must:	If the researcher decides to use *secondary data*, then he or she must:
1. decide where to collect data;	1. trust the data collection occurred properly;
2. decide from whom to collect data;	2. trust the data was organized properly;
3. decide what questions to ask and how to ask these questions;	3. trust the questions were answered properly; and
4. decide how much data to collect;	4. trust the sample is appropriate.
5. decide how to analyze the data collected;	
6. decide how to measure or categorize the data;	
7. decide how to interpret the measurements or categories; and	
8. decide how to discuss the interpretation of the findings.	

also runs the risk of contaminating the data or biasing the data that he or she is collecting. His or her presence in the group might steer the group in a direction that it never would have considered without the input of the participant observer.

Quantitative researchers are concerned about what they consider the subjective nature of qualitative research, and qualitative researchers are worried about the lack of context that numbers provide, especially numbers that could have been manipulated at the operational stage when the researcher was establishing the protocol for measuring the variables of interest. Despite these challenges to both methods, each has much to offer. Quantitative researchers can provide breadth, while qualitative researchers can provide depth. Together, the two methodologies can provide a much more complete picture of the issues being

investigated. The use of mixed methodologies has grown steadily over the last two decades. One study that utilized both methods successfully is the *Welfare, Children and Families: A Three City Study* (1999).

A third option to quantitative and qualitative research is to conduct **experimental** research, but this rarely happens in sociology today, because of the ethical challenges that such social-psychological research poses. Since the study population is usually human subjects, it is challenging to create experimental and control groups and then make sure the control group was not exposed to the same things the experimental group was exposed to. The only way to achieve that would be to sequester the control group or the experimental group or both. This is not likely and even if it were generally acceptable, it would be very costly

Develop a Research Plan

In Sociological Application 1.1, you were asked to respond to call for action in your community. Before you think about making a significant change or helping your local community, you will need to assess the problem by gathering and analyzing information about the issue and people involved. Using the social issue identified in Sociological Application 1.1, develop a research plan to learn facts and prove or disprove your predictions. Following the scientific method outlined in this module, explain your research plan.

1. **Choose a Topic; Identify a Social Problem.**

   - Describe the issue you will study. In describing the social problem, specify who will be included in the target group or sample of your study.

2. **Create operational definitions for your initial or abstract concepts**

   - Develop a research question specifying independent and dependent variables.

3. **Check for validity**

   - Provide justification explaining how variables are operational or measurable.

4. **Find 5–10 scholarly articles on your topic and summarize three relevant studies (write one paragraph for each of the three studies)**

   - Visit the campus library and use the academic search engine such as EBSCOHOST and use Boolean Basics (key word searches) to research your topic.

   - Write down the complete reference citation in ASA style format for the three studies you summarized so your audience will be able to find the sources you used (refer to http://www.asanet.org/documents/teaching/pdfs/Quick_Tips_for_ASA_Style.pdf).

5. **Formulate a Hypothesis about two or more variables related to your topic.**

   - Make sure your hypothesis answers your research question (i.e., what relationship between variables do you believe you will find based on the knowledge you gained from reviewing other research studies on the issue).

6. **Create a plan for obtaining a random sample**

   - Provide justification for selecting the subgroup you will be sampling.

   - Explain how your sampling technique ensures every member of the population has an opportunity to participate in the study.

7. **Design a tool (i.e., questionnaire/survey) for collecting data**

   - Include a description of the research method (e.g., survey, questionnaire, interview, ethnography, etc.) you will use to collect data for your study and explain why the method you chose is most appropriate to gather information about your research question.

   - Develop your research instrument to be used to collect data from your study participants.

8. **Address challenges or limitations you might encounter when implementing your plan**

   - Explain the ethical issues (pitfalls/problems) involved in gathering evidence about your topic. What measures will you use to protect confidentiality and anonymity, avoid plagiarism and falsification of data, and ensure the integrity of your research?

to manage such an experiment. The 1971 *Stanford Prison Experiment* (https://www.youtube.com/watch?v=R8A6JhU8VFc) implemented experimental research protocols but was terminated after six days because of the psychological stress the environment created on the student participants.

These three types of research design: survey, observation, and experiment are each considered as a form of **primary analysis**. Conducting primary analysis means one is conducting original research, establishing the protocols, obtaining a random sample, analyzing the data, and interpreting the findings. This process is labor intensive, time consuming, and expensive. Frequently, the resources to conduct this type of research are not available, so many researchers opt to engage in secondary analysis. This can take a variety of forms. Most researchers who conduct primary data analysis accept grants from public and private agencies and, as a result of accepting these funds, they agree to make the data available to the public a few years after the initial release of the data. This gives the public access to a variety of rich data such as the U.S. Census, the Panel Study of Income Dynamics (PSID), the Current Population Survey (CPS), the General Social Survey (GSS), the Multi-City Study of Urban Inequality (MCSUI), and many other sources. Secondary data analysis can also take the form of turning everyday items into data. Magazine covers, television episodes or newscasts, and music videos can become data to be analyzed. Well-known family researcher Ralph LaRossa and his colleagues (2000) turned comic strips into data when he analyzed how fathers were depicted in comic strips.

References

Best, Joel. 2001. *Damned Lies and Statistics*. Oakland, CA: University of California Press.

Doll, Jonathan Jacob, Zohreh Eslami, and Lynne Walters. 2013. "Understanding Why Students Drop Out of High School, According to Their Own Reports: Are They Pushed or Pulled, or Do They Fall Out? A Comparative Analysis of Seven Nationally Representative Studies." *SAGE Open* October–December 2013:1–15.

Franke, Richard Herbert and James D. Kaul. 1978. "The Hawthorne Experiments: First Statistical Interpretation." *American Sociological Review* 43: 623–643.

Hudson, Lisa. 2008. "Real Numbers: Connecting Jobs to Education." Issues in Science and Technology 24 (4, Summer). Retrieved from http://issues.org/24-4/realnumbers-25/.

LaRossa, Ralph, Charles Jaret, Malati Gadgil, and G. Robert Wynn. 2000. "The Changing Culture of Fatherhood in Comic-Strip Families: A Six Decade Analysis." *Journal of Marriage and Family* 62: 375–387.

Michaelis, David. 2008. *Schultz and Peanuts: A Biography*. New York: Harper Perennial.

Mills, C. Wright. 1959. *The Sociological Imagination*. New York: Oxford University Press.

Neuman, Laurence W. 2009. *Understanding Research*. Boston, MA: Allyn & Bacon.

Richards, Emily and Dave Terkanian. 2013. "Occupational Employment Projections to 2022." *Monthly Labor Review*, December. Retrieved from http://www.bls.gov/opub/mlr/2013/article/occupational-employment-projections-to-2022.htm.

Shyrock, Henry and Jacon Siegel. 1976. *Methods and Materials of Demography* (condensed by Edward G. Stockwell). San Diego, CA: Academic Press.

Stack, Carol. 1974. *All Our Kin*. New York: Harper and Row.

U.S. Department of Education, National Center for Education Statistics. 2015. *The Condition of Education 2015* (NCES 2015-144), Status Dropout Rates. Retrieved from https://nces.ed.gov/programs/digest/d14/tables/dt14_219.70.asp.

U.S. Department of Health and Human Services, Administration for Children and Families, Administration on Children, Youth and Families, Children's Bureau. 2015. *Child maltreatment 2013*. Retrieved from http://www.acf.hhs.gov/programs/cb/research-data-technology/statistics-research/child-maltreatment.

Valentine, Bettylou. 1978. *Hustling and Other Hard Work: Lifestyles in the Ghetto*. New York: The Free Press.

Winston Pamela, Ronald Angel, Linda Burton, P. Lindsay Chase-Lansdale, Andrew Cherlin, Robert Moffitt, William Julius Wilson. 1999. *Welfare, Children, and Families: A Three-City Study, Overview and Design Report*. Available at http://web.jhu.edu/threecitystudy/images/overviewanddesign.pdf.

Do you know the terms?

Age cohort	Methodocentric
Biography	Microsociology
Categorical data	Numerical data
Causal logic	Objective data
Conflict theory	Operational definition
Convenience sample	Personal problems
Demography	Primary analysis
Dependent variable	Qualitative research
Environmental theory	Quantitative research
Exchange theory	Random sample
Experimental research	Secondary analysis
Feminism	Social interventions
Five-step research process	Social location
Functionalism	Social problems
Hawthorne Effect	Sociological imagination
History	Spurious relationship
Independent variable	Subjective data
Latent function	Symbolic interactionism
Macrosociology	Theoretical paradigms
Manifest function	Validity

Using the list provided below, create a personal dictionary of key terms and concepts presented in this module. Include the term, phonetic spelling (if needed), and definition in your own words. Next, provide a real world example of the term or concept based on your previous knowledge or new information you learned in this module to help re-enforce learning.

MODULE 3

The Power of Culture

Culture and Identity

When we look at another person or if we ask another person to describe his or her culture, we start to form generalizations about that person's race, ethnicity, sex, religion, or birthplace. When people exchange cultural information, they tend to include a summary of customs, languages spoken, and traditions about food, clothing, and musical preferences. However, the way people describe their culture does not provide an adequate description of who they are or their identity. For example, if you learn someone is a "white Christian" or "black Muslim" or "Asian Buddhist," do you think you know who that person is? Your mind may start picturing who that person is, but you do not really know that specific individual. If one knows others simply by their religion and race, one cannot develop an accurate understanding about who they are, including how they think and live until one gets to know them, talks with them, and sees them for who they are as an individual. Using social group labels and cultural stereotypes to describe self and others creates relationships founded on assumptions and fallacies, limiting what people know about each other and how to perceive interactions. Moreover, this can be a cause for interpersonal misunderstanding and conflict.

The use of labels in self-identification reinforces power relationships between social groups. People become voyeurs or passive onlookers in the

©Rawpixel.com/Shutterstock.com

stories of each other's lives without the hands-on knowledge and tactile experience of living in their shoes (Collins 1998). Religion and racial group identification (as well as ethnicity, birthplace, customs, etc.) do not provide an accurate summation of the individual's culture, which goes beyond generalized labels and stereotypes.

Culture encompasses a person's overall identity including the values, beliefs, norms, language, and materials, which guide how people live. **Nonmaterial culture** is associated with values, beliefs, norms, and language, which influence how individuals think and behave, whereas **material culture** encompasses the objects, artifacts, or tools people have made or use to live. Throughout history, there

TABLE 3

Non-Material Culture				Material Culture
Values	**Beliefs**	**Norms**	**Language**	**Materials**
An ideal principle or standard of behavior	Faith or confidence in someone or something	Formal or informal rules	Spoken, written or symbolic forms of communication	Possessions, goods, and structures
Examples:	Examples:	Examples:	Examples:	Examples:
• Equality • Freedom • Love	• God • Superstition • Reincarnation	• Drinking alcohol • Smoking tobacco • Shaking hands	• Ebonics • Numbers • Images	• Clothing • Cell phones • Buildings

FIGURE 11

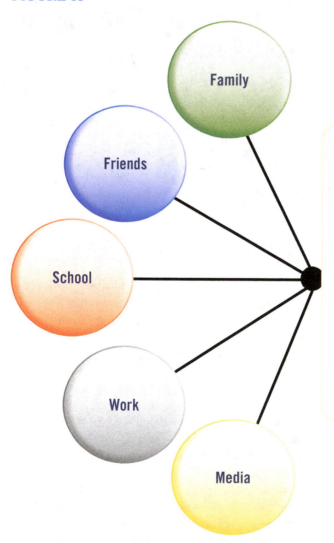

Cultural Identity

Age
Education
Ethnicity
Family
Sex
Gender
Health
Place of Birth
Geographic Location
Linguistic Diversity
Physical and Mental Ability
Race
Religion
Social Class

Courtesy Vera Kennedy.

have always been differences between how people believe they should live (**ideal culture**) and how they actually live (**real culture**).

Culture is learned and passed down from one generation to the next. People learn values, beliefs, norms, language, and materials of significance from the cultural groups to which they belong. It takes more than one introduction or a few encounters to learn and understand someone's culture. The power of culture resonates from a variety of elements that constitute a person's identity. One's ethnic background—for example, being of Mexican descent—is only one characteristic that shapes identity. A person's age, education, family, sex, gender, health, place of birth, geographic location, linguistic diversity, physical and mental ability, religion, physical and mental ability, sexual orientation, and social class also shape the development of a person's cultural identity. These various dimensions of ourselves intersect to make us the unique individuals that we are and affect both how we perceive ourselves as well as how others perceive us.

The cultural explanations received and reenforced by family, friends, school, work, and media justify the cultural realities in which people live. Individuals assume many aspects of culture are "natural" or "normal"; however, realities are socially constructed and transferred from one person to another as they are understood and interpreted. People create and define various aspects of life and how individuals live.

Words, symbols, and ideas are created by people to communicate, share information, and assign meaning. Even "facts" are socially and culturally constructed. They are derived from shared, proven, and accepted truths. Mathematics and physics are prime examples of how socially and culturally accepted truths become facts. Both disciplines are used to explain the relationship and influence of nature on life, but, as with all other academic disciplines, explanations are formed from a perspective of human understanding and interpretation and may be bound by time or place. This explains why, at a particular time in human history, most people believed the world was flat. Similarly, most people once believed the modern human race comprised many species which now, in light of new data gathered from recent discoveries using new technology, has not been proven, changing the socially and culturally accepted truth or fact. While three or four species of hominin did exist at the same time and place two million years ago, modern *Homo sapiens*, Neandertals, and Denisovans are generally considered members of the same species because "there has been extensive admixture [i.e., interbreeding] across modern humans for tens of thousands of years, and at least some admixture across several archaic groups" (Antrosio 2012:1; Hawks 2016). People define life and instruct others on how to live (i.e., culture) from information passed on to them or learned by them which they believe is personally and socially true.

Cultural universals or common cultural elements are found throughout society (e.g., birth, death, war, crime, etc.). The differences in culture are determined by the customs groups use in viewing or approaching these universals. For example, cultural groups throughout the world understand death as a loss of life, but each group has different perspectives and practices to view and deal with death including dressing of the body, funeral, burial, and cremation (see *Customs and Religious Protocols* at http://www.amemory-tree.co.nz/customs.php).

"We're not hibernating this year. Too much cultural change to keep up with."

©Cartoonresource/Shutterstock.com

Though technology transforms society, culture does not change rapidly. **Cultural lag** refers to the amount of time for cultural changes to occur. Generally, material culture changes before other cultural aspects of society. Sometimes, material culture, such as "High Definition-HD or Blu-ray Discs," catches on and sometimes not (e.g., 3D televisions and digital downloads). Some people are more open to change in the form of technology or material possessions than others, but they may still be reluctant to adapt or alter core values, beliefs, and norms, including the words, symbols, and meanings associated with them. For example, people are more likely to adapt to new communication devices and fashions long before they alter their perspectives on immigration, gay marriage, and redistribution of wealth.

Contact and interactions between diverse groups creates **cultural diffusion** inducing cultural change and often promoting Western ideals and capitalism. Technological advances have improved travel and communications influencing the diffusion of a consumer culture across groups worldwide creating a shared culture. For example, *Disneyland* has now become *Walt Disney Parks and Resorts Worldwide, Inc.*, featuring similarly-themed amusement parks in Los Angeles, California; Orlando, Florida; Paris, France; Hong Kong; Shanghai, China; and Tokyo, Japan. The process where cultures in different locations are becoming similar to one another is called **cultural leveling**. The growth of cultural leveling generates global unification and political unity at the loss of diverse, unique, and indigenous cultures or cultural diversity.

Since culture is embedded in all aspects of people's lives, we have a tendency to judge others from our cultural viewpoint or ethnocentric perspective. **Ethnocentrism** builds group cohesiveness for people who share the same cultural point of view; however, it leads to discrimination against people who have different cultural perceptions and behaviors. When people are exposed to a culture different from their own, they experience discomfort and sometimes shock as a result of recognizable differences in behaviors and cultural practices. For example, in the United States people have guinea pigs as pets. When someone

from the United States visits Peru, they may be shocked, disgusted, or offended to be served guinea pig as a meal though it is one of the primary sources protein for people in Peru. Another example is the acceptance of public decapitations for death row inmates in Saudi Arabia compared to lethal injections in the United States.

Differences in core values or beliefs are perceived as threatening to individuals and reinforce ethnocentric views. A strong connection to core values or beliefs blinds individuals to social reality and can prevent acceptance of other cultural groups. **Imperialism**, a form of ethnocentrism, is practiced worldwide as an effort to bring one dominant cultural interest into power over another. Typically, this practice is utilized among nations and governments to maintain a dominant culture and unified core values supporting the existing power structure. Examples of cultural imperialism in the United States include the country's oppressive treatment and relationship with its indigenous people (i.e., Native Americans), the acceptance of racial slavery until the passage of the Thirteenth Amendment in 1865, racial segregation in the form of "Jim Crow" laws up through the 1960s, and, until recently, laws prohibiting gay marriage.

Contrary to ethnocentrism, **culture relativism** considers a person's values and behaviors from the perspective of that's person's own culture, not our own. This means we seek to understand others' beliefs and activities in terms of their cultural contexts. Cultural relativism judges people on their own cultural terms, which reinforces an open-minded perspective towards different cultural groups. However, the danger of this perspective is in allowing individuals and groups the latitude to violate human rights or other conduct harmful practices (e.g., female genital cutting and female circumcision) under the protection of their cultural values, beliefs, or norms. Just because something is a norm or an accepted practice in one culture, does that mean it should be allowed, accepted, or even respected by other cultures?

Social problems arise from differences in culture. People misuse identity labels to describe certain groups or individuals as a social problem rather than discuss the social arrangements and structure responsible for the problem itself. The condition or problem becomes associated with a social group rather than the inadequate, dysfunctional, or absent social arrangement or any problem with the existing social structure. For example, poverty is seen as an individual problem or a problem of a specific group of people rather than resulting from a lack of jobs, substandard wages, a lack of affordable housing, high costs of health care, etc. Placing a condition label on a group of people as a social problem establishes a power structure where those labeled as the "problem" become oppressed and in need of being fixed, cured, or even eradicated by others. Wes Kim (2012) produced a short video entitled Vision Test to show how Americans focus on division and differences re-enforcing cultural stereotypes and positions of power (https://youtu.be/jS86dY9-5zg).

Disneyland Park

Disneyland Park was established in Anaheim July 17, 1955, featuring Sleeping Beauty Castle

https://en.wikipedia.org/wiki/Disneyland

https://en.wikipedia.org/wiki/Tokyo _Disneyland#/media/File:TDL_Cinderella _Castle_New_Color.jpg

Tokyo Disneyland

Tokyo Disneyland was established April 15, 1983, featuring Cinderella Castle

https://en.wikipedia.org/wiki/Tokyo_Disneyland

https://en.wikipedia.org/wiki/Tokyo _Disneyland#/media/File:TDL_Cinderella _Castle_New_Color.jpg

Walt Disney World Resort

Walt Disney World Resort was established in Orlando, Florida, October 1, 1971, featuring Cinderella Castle

https://en.wikipedia.org/wiki/Walt_Disney_World

https://en.wikipedia.org/wiki/Walt_Disney _World#/media/File:Cinderella_Castle_at_ Magic_Kingdom.jpg

Disneyland Paris

Disneyland Paris was established April 12, 1992, featuring Le Château de la Belle au Bois Dormant (i.e., The Castle of Sleeping Beauty)

https://en.wikipedia.org/wiki/Disneyland_Paris

https://en.wikipedia.org/wiki/Disneyland_Park_ (Paris)#/media/File:Sleeping_Beauty_Castle,_Dis- neyland,_Paris.jpg

Disneyland Hong Kong

Disneyland Hong Kong was established September 12, 2005, featuring Sleeping Beauty Castle

https://en.wikipedia.org/wiki/ Hong_Kong_Disneyland

https://en.wikipedia.org/wiki/Hong_Kong _Disneyland#/media/File:Disney_in_star.jpg

Disneyland Resort Shanghai

Disneyland Resort Shanghai was established June 16, 2016, featuring The Enchanted Storybook Castle

https://en.wikipedia.org/wiki/ Shanghai_Disney_Resort

https://en.wikipedia.org/wiki/ Shanghai_Disneyland_Park

Social Issues

Race Relations

At the center of discussions about **race** and race relations is the concept of "race" itself. The manner in which the concept was defined was flawed for so long. For years, biological definitions dominated explanations of race (Banton 1987). Today it is generally agreed that race is a socially-constructed concept based on physical characteristics or phenotype (Omi and Winant 1994; Machery and Faucher 2005). Although the notion that race is a biological construct still persists in the way that the term is applied and understood, the fact of the matter is that race does not exist under a microscope. The genetic variation among members of any so-called "race" are greater that the various between members of different so called "races." In fact, human beings are genetically among the most similar of all living species on the planet (see http://www.pbs.org/race). Still, despite the evidence that "race" is not real and that it is just an idea we have ascribed to biology, because "race" has been treated as biologically real for so long, now there are real consequences associated with it, and people's behaviors are impacted by their perceptions.

RACE LITERACY

Test your "Race Literacy" by taking an online Genetic Diversity Quiz at http://www.pbs.org/race/000_About/002_04_a-godeeper.htm.

Race is a concept of convenience. The racial categories most often used are "umbrella terms" which cover a wide range of diverse groups. In the United States, many racial/ethnic groups are classified together under five umbrellas: White/European American, Black/African American, Hispanic/Latino American, Asian American, and Native American. One clue that race is not real is that so many groups are lumped together under these umbrellas, even though most do not see themselves as one entity and these groups are quite distinct from each other with regard to various aspects of culture, including language, religion, music, food, etc. For example, the term Hispanic/Latino is used to refer to people from Mexico, other parts of Central America, such as Costa Ricans, Guatemalans, Hondurans, Nicaraguans, Panamanians, and Salvadorans, and throughout South America, including Argentinians, Bolivians, Chileans, Colombians, Ecuadorians, Peruvians, and Venezuelans.

A second clue to the idea of "race" being an illusion is that racial classifications of these groups vary significantly from one country to another. For example, what is considered "white" in Brazil is not often considered "white" in the United States. Another clue is the oversimplification of the classifications. Not everyone fits nicely into the categories. For example, where do people from the Middle East fit? What exactly is a white or black person? Are there actually people whose skin is white or black? No. Still, though, the power of the concept of race is real. Despite a recognition of how narrow the typical textbook examination of racial groups is, most scholarly examinations reproduce this culture by presenting each racial group as a monolithic entity that must be examined in its totality. Every so often, a post-racial position on matters of race relations is assumed, based on the false belief that a person's race no longer matters. However, such arguments are usually met by calls to perpetuate the classifications and umbrella terms as flawed as they may be, because, at least by capturing the false concept, it is possible to measure differential treatment and outcomes. Without capturing data for the false racial categories, no case for addressing racial group disparities can be made. As much as some segments of society want to embrace a post-racial culture, the current culture cannot support this because for so long it has treated race as is if it makes a difference and so it does. A person's racial classification plays a critical role in determining access to so many resources (Feagin and Sikes 1994). We have treated members of different racial categories as if they are considerably different beings, rather than beings that share most of their genetic material (Machery and Faucher

2005). The small difference or variation in genetic material and phenotypes is mostly due to adaptations to the environment. For example, the closer to the equator your ancestors came from, the more likely your skin is to have dark melanin. Consequently, although geography is a better explanatory variable for human differences than "race," we have built an entire infrastructure of language and ideology about race, which has been used to justify the institution of racial slavery for Africans and African Americans and the unequal and oppressive treatment of Native Americans and Mexicans and Mexican Americans among other groups.

Racial Profiling

Racial profiling is a term used to describe relying primarily or solely on a person's perceived "race" or ethnicity to determine whether their behavior warrants investigation by police officers, but this practice can take place in other contexts as well. Typically, this practice involves prejudicial assumptions based on physical features or phenotype associated with "race," such as skin color, hair type, and facial features, and/or cultural clothing (e.g., "hoodies" and turbans). Dealing with this form of discrimination has been challenging, because systematic data on the race of citizens stopped by police is not always collected. Due to growing concerns about racial profiling, more and more police departments are keeping such records (Weitzer and Tuch 2002), but the method of collecting such information varies and can be very subjective. For example, who determines the "race" of the driver—the officer or the driver? Even once the driver's race is "identified," how does one prove that race was the primary or determining factor for the police to make the stop? Despite these challenges, numerous studies have revealed increased likelihood for people being pulled over by police if they are black or brown (sometimes referred to as Driving While Black or Brown or DWB) (ACLU 2008; Harris 1999; Warren, Tomaskovic-Devey, Smith, Zingraff, and Mason 2006).

Much of the problem with racial profiling stems from attitudes regarding its practice. Most police departments report having no problem in this area. Public sentiment is divided along racial lines. Racial minorities express major concerns about a problem that impacts their lives on a regular, sometimes even daily, basis. White Americans tend to see the issue of racial profiling as less problematic. Although White Americans recognize racial profiling is a problem, they do tend to believe it is a not problem in their community. Furthermore, when police do engage in profiling racial minorities, white Americans frequently express that they feel such treatment is justified because racial minorities are more likely to be involved in activities that warrant more attention from the police (Tuch and Weitzer 1997; Weitzer 1999, 2000; Weitzer and Tuch 1999, 2002).

The face of racial profiling changed considerably following the attacks on the World Trade Center on September 11, 2001. The 9/11 attacks prompted widespread hysteria among the public and some officials which led many Muslim Americans and others, particularly Sikh Americans, who were mistakenly identified as Muslim Americans to be treated as potential threats (Bakalian and Bozorgmehr 2009). This was not the first time an act of violence against the United States has led to large scale racial profiling of American citizens. After Japan attacked Pearl Harbor during WWII, Japanese Americans were placed in internment camps with little to no cause to justify placing them there (Takaki 2012).

©Rena Schild/Shutterstock.com

Recently, several high profile cases—including Sandra Bland, Michael Brown, Eric Garner, Oscar Grant, Freddie Gray, Laquan McDonald, Walter Scott, and Tamir Rice—have called into question whether police are treating all citizens the same (see www.mappingpoliceviolence. org and http://www.washingtonpost.com/sf/national/2015/08/08/black-and-unarmed/). Many Americans, regardless of race, are concerned that racial minorities are not receiving the same benefit of the doubt that a white citizen might experience. The "Black Lives Matter" movement emerged due to concerns about racial bias in policing (www.blacklivesmatter.com). This movement challenges us as a society to consider that if we are products of a culture that has prejudice and discrimination embedded in it, then police officers are not immune to this prejudice and discrimination. If they are not immune, then they must receive cultural awareness training and this training must be ongoing, so that police officers and other members of the judicial system are aware of how potential biases, including hidden biases, might impact how they engage with citizens (Mooney 2014). Pushback against this movement has involved some characterizing the movement as divisive and proclaiming that "Blue Lives Matter" or "All Lives Matter." Others, such as conservative TV personality Elizabeth Hasselbeck and New Jersey's Republican Governor Chris Christie, have gone as far as calling the "Black Lives Matter" movement a "hate group" and suggesting that it encourages violence against the police (Blidner 2015; Hensch 2015). Leaders of the "Black Lives Matter" movement insist that they are not anti-police. They recognize that some fringe elements of the movement may participate in such activities, but the main goal of the movement is to bring awareness to racial bias in policing and to highlight the need for further cultural awareness training in the police community and the larger society, as well.

Color-Blind Racism

With the increasing diversification of the U.S. population, many people believe racial-ethnic differences are diminishing in America. Many suggest prejudice and discrimination towards people of color has decreased, and historically underrepresented minority groups now have equitable access to resources particularly economic success. Dinesh D'Souza of The American Enterprise Institute, author of *The End of Racism* ([1995] 1996), claims racism "no longer has the power to thwart blacks or any other group in achieving their economic, political, and social aspirations." This viewpoint re-enforces the perception that people of color in the United States are no longer disadvantaged when it comes to education, income, health, housing, and discrimination by social institutions including law enforcement, financial lenders and banks, and employers. However, current data reported by the U.S. Bureau of Labor Statistics (http://www.bls.gov/cps/cpsaat03.htm), U.S. Census Bureau (http://www.census.gov/hhes/www/housing/census/historic/racegraph.html), U.S. Department of Health and Human Services (http://www.cdc.gov/nchs/data/hus/hus13.pdf), and Bureau of Justice Statistics (http://www.bjs.gov/content/pub/pdf/p14.pdf) verify continued discrepancies in homeownership, incarceration rates, educational attainment, employment, occupation, and earnings for people of color.

Color-blind racism refers to subtle prejudicial attitudes and discriminatory behaviors by individuals, groups, and institutions towards people of color. Eduardo Bonilla-Silva (2009) explains color-blind racism occurs when people use excuses

©Rena Schild/Shutterstock.com

to justify racial differences, inequity, and separation by believing racism is a thing of the past and does not influence people of color today. The term "color-blind" suggests people no longer see racial-ethnic differences or treat others differently as a result race and ethnicity, understating the differences in privilege, status, and power experienced by people of color. Color-blind racism allows people to believe disadvantages among people of color are a result of individualism and personal choice reflecting an ideology that racism is a myth.

Color-blind ideology ignores the existence of race privilege constructs in society. However, **white privilege** is a historically common experience for people of white, European descent in the United States who enter the world as members of the dominant group. Whites have always made the rules, benefitted from the rules, and continue to be the group with the greatest wealth in the nation (Wise 2005). White privilege provides whites with an advantage and place of belonging upon birth, unlike people of color who must prove themselves deserving of equity and privilege.

Minority Success and Cultural Capital

By acknowledging the social conditions experienced by people of color in comparison with whites, we are able to view how their experiences

©Ollyy/*Shutterstock.com*

differ. There is no equity in opportunity or life chances for people of color when the social systems, institutions, processes, thinking, and behavior of society do not reflect an equal experience for all. Ellis Cose (1993) in his book *The Rage of the Privileged Class* documented the experiences of successful African Americans to show discrepancies in earning recognition and achievement. His findings show people of color must acculturate and develop the cultural capital necessary for social mobility and success.

Cultural capital refers to assets, knowledge, and/or skills of social origin including values, beliefs, norms, language, and materials accumulated and transmitted by socializing agents (Bourdieu 1991). According to Bridge (2006), cultural capital is developed in three forms: 1) institutionalized capital or formal learning; 2) objectified capital including arts, literature, and music; and 3) embodied capital or dispositions built from social exposure. Similar to other forms of capital, the larger the investment, the greater the return. This explains why whites are accustomed to the dominant culture and acclimate to the formal and informal rules of societal success and achievement. In contrast, people of color with dissimilar cultural capital face social inequalities integrating into the dominant culture and achieving success (Reay 2004).

According to Cose (1993), the most common issues confronted by people of color on their way to success are the inability to fit in, lack of respect, low expectations, faint praise, maintaining an identity congruent with their own race while attempting to fit in with the white dominant ruling class, self-censorship on sensitive topics regarding race when they are raised, collective guilt for the bad or unproductive behaviors of others from their own race, and exclusion from the club or "good ol' boy" network. These experiences demonstrate how people of color and whites may live different lives and achieve and obtain varying degrees of success.

Immigration

Diversity is a frequent topic of conversation, and it is treated as an asset in some settings such as college campuses and many workplaces. This was not always the case. The road to embracing racial and ethnic diversity has been filled with many challenges. For most of its history, the United States of America has encouraged assimilation and the "melting pot" has been used as a metaphor to describe a substitutive process in which one "substitutes" American culture for one's ethnic culture of origin. In this model, difference is minimized and homogeneity is the goal. This paradigm was widely accepted and rarely challenged, but over time people did begin to ask why they have to divest themselves of what makes

©Chad Zuber/Shutterstock.com

them unique in order to be accepted as truly "American." Yinger (1994) and Jendian (2008) argue that assimilation can also be an "additive" process or, what Hurh and Kim (1983) call, "adhesive adaptation," in which an individual may adopt mainstream cultural traits in addition to one's own ethnic values, norms, and styles. Now that diversity is considered an asset rather than a liability, many more people in the United States of America are embracing multiculturalism or a pluralistic perspective.

Although immigration to the United States has always been constant throughout the country's history, some structure and boundaries or restrictions have been in place to manage the amount and types of immigration allowed, resulting in distinct waves of immigration (Martin 2013; Massey 1995). The first significant "wave," sometimes referred to as the "old immigration," occurred between 1820 and 1880 and consisted predominantly of immigrants from Northern and Western Europe (e.g., England and Germany among other countries). A second wave of immigrants entered the United States between 1880 and 1924, and consisted predominantly of immigrants from Southern and Eastern Europe (e.g., Italy, Greece, and Russia among other countries) and were notably different than the first two waves in terms of their phenotype, religious practices, language, and general customs. In response to this wave, Nativists and descendants of the first wave of immigrants created a new immigration policy that would control the entry of immigrants and give the advantage to immigrants hailing from Northern and Western European countries.

The National Origins System was established in 1921 and this new system culminated with the passage of the Immigration Act of 1924, which established a quota system for determining who could enter the United States. Under this new system, each country could send 2% of the current total number of people of that national origin living in the United States as of the 1890 census (Martin 2013). Clearly, during the third wave of immigration from 1924 to 1965, the number of immigrants from Northern and Western European countries was far greater than the number from Southern and Eastern European countries. This quota system would ensure the numbers would favor the Northern and Western Europeans. This National Origins System was in place until 1965, when it was replaced by the Immigration and Nationality Act of 1965, which ushered in the fourth and current wave of immigration to the United States. The fourth wave consists of immigrants from mostly Latin America and Asia. The quota system in place for the prior four and half decades restricted migration from these regions, but it was not the United States' first foray into exclusionary immigration policies; the Chinese Exclusion Act of 1882 prevented migration from Asia in general.

This fourth wave of immigration to the United States has lasted for 50 years already and there is no sign of its end. Some scholars suggest that the length of this wave has led to some backlash against immigrants (Massey 1995). They argue that there were breaks after the first few waves, which allowed them to become integrated into society before the next wave arrived, but with this continuous fourth wave, it is like a new wave is arriving year after year. The concerns about immigration are numerous. But, most of the discussion of immigration to the United States centers on efforts to control "illegal" or undocumented immigration. For a long time, immigration was considered a regional issue, because it was mostly border states and key entry states such as New York and California that had to deal with high levels of immigrant populations, both documented and undocumented. Now, most states have fairly sizeable and growing immigrant populations and they are dealing with the same issues that states that have long had sizeable immigrant populations have, such as bilingual education, perceived economic threats to native born workers, tax contributions, and utilization of public goods and services.

Debates continue to center around how to control immigration without stifling the process responsible for what many believe to be the country's best asset—its diversity (Martin 2013). Two strategies are dominating the current discussion on immigration. One calls for focusing on more enforcement strategies by investing more heavily in U.S. - Mexico border patrol and requiring employers to collect more data from potential hires to ensure they are authorized to work in the United States. The opposition wants to focus on "comprehensive immigration reform," which will focus on enforcement, but also provide "a path to legal immigrant status" (Martin 2013). Focusing on border control may not be the most effective way to handle illegal immigration because most undocumented immigrants entered the United States legally and became "illegal immigrants" when their visas and other documents expired ("Ten Myths about Immigration" [2011] 2015). Most evidence suggests that the borders are secure in most places, but individuals determined to enter will continue to breach security until they are successful. This usually involves crossing in less secure but dangerous areas such as the Arizona border (Waller Meyers 2006). It is also important, when considering how many resources to invest in controlling the flow of immigration to the United States, to recognize that the number of unauthorized immigrants has stabilized in recent years (Passel and Cohn 2015).

Gender and Sexuality

Upon birth, children are socialized based on the context of their **sex** or biological composition (e.g., reproductive organs and body structure). Despite the fact that some individuals are "intersex"—i.e., born with sex characteristics of both male and females—American society predominantly considers there to be only two sexes.

©Fosin/Shutterstock.com

Furthermore, the socialization process nurtures both self and social identity, promoting the development of **gender** identity, including the cultural and psychological characteristics associated with being female or male. Gender is a social construct and people create the roles and behaviors we teach girls and boys. For example, girls are encouraged to be nurturing, sensitive, and empathetic. In contrast, boys are encouraged to be assertive, independent, and aggressive. Even when parents attempt de-emphasize a particular pattern of socialization for their daughters and sons to help their children develop roles and behaviors across genders, society re-enforces gender norms based on sex through socialization in schools, work, and media.

Part of a person's sex or biological composition is their **sexual orientation**. Some people believe sexual orientation is nurtured or socialized; however, the chemical and biological reactions that occur within an individual causing sexual desire and arousal are not consciously controlled (Goleman 1988). The human condition is as much a part of nature as it is nurture. There are responses to being human that cannot be controlled either mentally or physically such as blinking when an object is thrown at your face or hunger pains in your stomach when your body needs nourishment. The sexual attraction and arousal one feels towards another person is a chemical and biological response. The ability to control acting on attraction or arousal is nurture, and people learn through the socialization process the appropriate time, place, and situation to behave sexually.

Beyond the Gender Binary

Gender conformity is engrained in society. People refer to each other using a pronoun (e.g., a female is referred to as she/her and a male as he/him) based on someone's assigned birth sex, not their gender identity or expression. In the gender binary structure, gender identity and sexual orientation are also associated with one's sex. Those whose gender identity and expression match their assigned birth sex are the norm, falling within the social conventions, power hierarchies, and traditions of the socially-accepted gender binary categories. They live with the privileges of being **cisgender** (see Figure 12).

How a person feels internally and how they express themselves externally does not always coincide with their assigned birth sex or gender label. For some, gender identity and gender expression do not fall under the "female" or "male" category nor do they not align with their assigned birth sex. We refer to these individuals as **transgender** because they live beyond the gender binary where the binary categories may not match neatly fall into one gender label or another (see Figure 13).

Violence and hate crimes against transgender people and others who identify and express themselves beyond the socially-accepted gender binary norms occur as a lack of understanding and awareness by the cisgender community. In 2015, Human Rights Campaign published "Addressing Anti-Transgender Violence," exploring realities, challenges, and solutions for policymakers and community advocates (http://hrc-assets.s3-website-us-east-1.amazonaws.com//files/assets/resources/HRC-AntiTransgenderViolence-0519.pdf). According to the Bureau of Justice Statistics, approximately 13% of hate crimes reported in 2012 resulted from offenders' perceptions and bias about the victim's sexual orientation (Wilson 2014). Considering over 98,000 hate crimes were recorded by law enforcement in 2012, this means

FIGURE 12

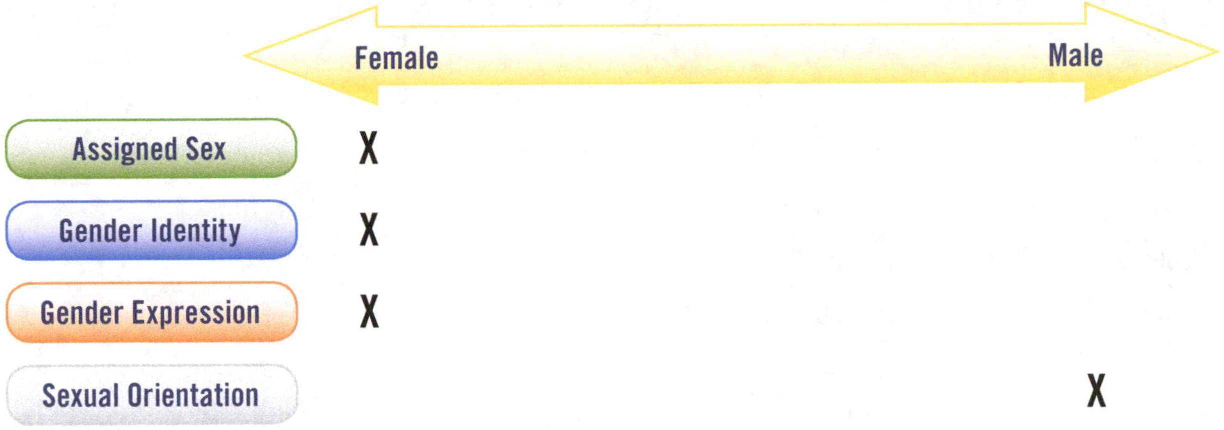

	Female	Male
Assigned Sex	X	
Gender Identity	X	
Gender Expression	X	
Sexual Orientation		X

Courtesy Vera Kennedy.

FIGURE 13

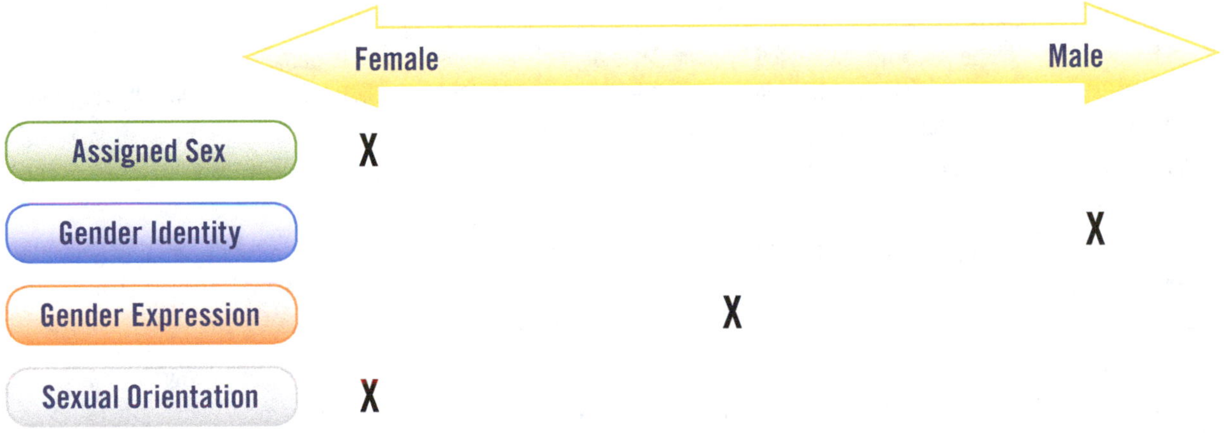

	Female		Male
Assigned Sex	X		
Gender Identity			X
Gender Expression		X	
Sexual Orientation	X		

Courtesy Vera Kennedy.

over 12,000 hate crimes were associated with a victim's sexual orientation that year.

In a 2012 study on heterosexuals' attitudes and perceptions of transgender people, researchers found prejudicial patterns consistent with other sexual minorities, including gay men, lesbians, and bisexuals, though transgender people were perceived significantly more negatively (Norton and Herek 2012). The study identified psychological authoritarianism, political conservatism, anti-egalitarianism, and religiosity (for women) as key factors influencing their sexual prejudice. Additionally, Norton and Herek (2012) found attitudes towards transgender people varied according to extent of personal contact with sexual minorities. If someone knows someone who is gay, lesbian, bisexual, and/or transgender, he or she is more likely to accept those in the sexual minority and challenge traditional notions of gender.

Pornography

The internet has created a global marketplace for creating, distributing, and selling pornographic materials. The porn industry no longer needs large production studios or storefronts to develop and disseminate products. Technology now allows people to produce and disseminate photos and images with cellular phones, tablets,

TABLE 4

Hate Crime Victimizations Recorded by the NCVS and UCR, 2004–2012			
	NCVS/a		
Year	Not Reported to Police	Reported to Police	UCR/b
2004	148,020	127,390	9,310
2005	116,500	101,940	9,170
2006	122,120	108,370	9,230
2007	152,680	110,760	9,590
2008	155,090	111,550	9,610
2009	171,150	113,470	9,010
2010	189,390	83,710	8,270
2011	161,970	53,970	7,960
2012	177,130	98,460	7,440

Note: Hate crimes include incidents confirmed by police as bias-motivated and incidents perceived by victims to be bias-motivated because the offender used hate language or left behind hate symbols. Estimates based on two-year rolling averages centered on the most recent year. Numbers rounded to the nearest ten.

a/The number of hate crime victimizations for which it was unknown whether the police were notified (6% or less) is not shown in table.

b/Includes murder/non-negligent manslaughter, forcible rape, aggravated assault, simple assault, intimidation, other crimes against persons, robbery, burglary, larceny-theft, motor vehicle theft, arson, destruction/vandalism, other crimes against property, and crimes against society. Excludes crimes against juveniles.

Source: Bureau of Justice Statistics, based on files provided by the FBI, Uniform Crime Reporting Program, Hate Crime Statistics, 2003–2012; and National Crime Victimization Survey, 2003–2012.

and other mobile devices using free and low cost editing software. Numerous websites sell products including gonzo pornography or live stream interactive shows where the viewer is placed in the scene by the performer acknowledging the camera and addressing the viewer directly.

People from throughout the world are now able to access pornographic videos, images, and explicit materials using an electronic device and the worldwide web at any place and any time with wifi or internet connectivity. The accessibility of porn has increased its use and concern for the influence of explicit images on personal and social development. Data from the national Youth Internet Safety Survey examined a cross-sectional sample of children and adolescents ages 10–17 and found 87% of youth 14 years or older reported looking at sexual images online (Ybarra and Mitchell 2005). These adolescents were more likely to report clinical signs of depression and low levels of emotional bonding with their caregivers. A 2008 study of more than 500 college students identified the age and gender of online pornographic seekers. Approximately 93% of males and 62% of females were exposed to online pornography during adolescence (Sabina, Wolak, and Finkelhor 2008). Males were more likely to view pornography often and view extreme images such as rape and child pornography while females reported more involuntary exposure.

TABLE 5

Victims' Perceptions of Offender Bias in Hate Crimes, 2004, 2011, and 2012						
Offender Bias	2004		2011		2012	
Ethnicity/a	22	%	30	%	51	%
Race	58		58		46	
Association/b	23		40		34	
Religion	10		25		28	
Gender	12		25		26	
Sexual orientation	22		19	!	13	
Disability	11		22		11	
Perceived characteristics/c	19		15	!	7	!

Note: Hate crime includes incidents confirmed by police as bias-motivated and incidents perceived by victims to be bias-motivated because the offender used hate language or left behind hate symbols. Estimates based on two-year rolling averages centered on the most recent year. Detail does not sum to total due to victims reporting more than one type of bias motivating the hate-related victimizations.

! Interpret with caution; estimate based on 10 or fewer cases, or the coefficient of variation is greater than 50%.

a/Motivated by victim's ancestral, cultural, social, or national affiliation.

b/Motivated by victim's association with people having certain characteristics.

c/Motivated by offender's perception of victim's characteristics.

Source: Bureau of Justice Statistics, National Crime Victimization Survey, 2003–2012.

🔲 BE AN ALLY

- Do not assume someone who appears to look female wants to be referred to as "she/her" or a male as "he/him." Refer to people by the name they use when they introduce themselves.
- Before you ask someone about their birth sex, gender identity, gender expression, or sexual orientation ask yourself, "Would I want someone to ask me that?"
- Do not tolerate anti-transgender attitudes or behaviors they propagate—anxiety, fear, misconceptions, and myths; instead, build bridges to understanding and empathy by following "9 Healthy Ways to Communicate" (StirFry Seminars and Consulting 2009):
  1. Reflect back what is being said. Use their words, not yours.
  2. Begin where they are, not where you want them to be.
  3. Be curious and open to what they are trying to say.
  4. Notice what they are saying and what they are not.
  5. Emotionally relate to how they are feeling. Nurture the relationship.
  6. Notice how you are feeling. Be honest and authentic.
  7. Take responsibility for your part in the conflict or misunderstanding.
  8. Try to understand how their past affects who they are and how those experiences affect their relationship with you.
  9. Stay with the process and the relationship, not just the solution.

(Chong 2012)

©ayelet-keshet/ Shutterstock.com

to select hardcore pornography (e.g., child pornography, group sex, bodily and sexual distortions, humiliation and degradation, sex with animals, and bondage, torture, and violence) and increased a viewer's sexist attitudes. Overall, research on online pornography viewers found users correlate sexual relationships with aggression and develop sexual taste for overtly explicit images and videos depicting domination of a submissive without boundaries.

Rape in the Military

The U.S. military has faced many challenges in upholding a culture free of sexual assault. In 2012, the Department of Defense reported 3,374 cases of sexual assault among active service members. These incidences of abusive sexual contact and rape were 6% higher than in 2011. Exacerbating the issue has been the lack of victim care and offender accountability within the armed forces. Of the 3,374 cases of sexual assault, only 880 were determined "substantiated" by the military and received misconduct charges, ranging from court-martial to non-judicial punishment to administrative discharge to other adverse administrative actions. Major barriers to stopping sexual assault perpetrators and eliminating the code of silence among service members have included a lack of environmental conditions that create a safe place for reporting offenses and providing advocacy services and support to victims. Service members who have been violated are fearful of retaliation by commanding officers and other service members for reporting incidences. Find out more at http://www.pbs.org/now/shows/421/index.html.

A far more common issue often ignored by military forces is sex and rape during times of war. The exploitation of women intensifies during wartime. War brings more women into sex work, heightened by male sexuality, and war enhances domination-submission relationships where victorious soldiers express domination by raping conquered women (Goldstein 2001). Media glamorizes the deprived social and emotional outlets of soldiers in war films depicting sex-obsessed men

Regular viewing of online pornographic material into adulthood has revealed serious psychological conditions related to overexposure. Research has shown adult cyberpornography users lack social bonds and possess more antisocial and/or erotophilic personality traits than non-users (Stack, Wasserman, and Kern 2004; Shim, Lee, and Paul 2007). Zillmann and Bryant (1984) found repeated, extensive exposure (480 minutes over a six-week period) to pornography depicting women as hyperpromiscuous and as sexual objects resulted in the trivialization of sexual aggressiveness among online pornography users. Milburn, Mather, and Conrad (2000) found that viewing pornographic scenes containing sexually objectifying images resulted in an increased acceptance of rape myths and of attributing responsibility of a rape to the victim. In 2014, Shim and Paul showed cyberpornography users felt anonymous and expressed greater willingness

(Nielson 2015), so how this wage gap persists is not due to blatant acts of discrimination that were once legal. Instead, the wage gap is the result of several subtle processes. Of course, when women first entered the work force, it was acceptable to pay them lower wages than men, because they were presumed to be secondary earners in the household. This was not always the case then, and it certainly is no longer the case, since in many households today women are the primary and sole earners (Wang, Parker, and Taylor 2013). Minority women experience a double penalty because, not only are their wages less than men's wages, their wages are also lower than the wages of white women.

One of the main factors that perpetuates the wage gap is occupational segregation. A significant amount of work continues to be sex stereotyped. Due to ideological beliefs, work that involves "soft skills," such as caring for and nurturing others, is typically considered the domain of women, while work that involves physical labor, mechanics, or math and science skills is considered the domain of men. Structurally, industries that have more men in them pay more, although there is no evidence that the skills set required to perform the work in these industries is greater than that needed to perform the work in female-dominated industries (Hegewisch and Hartmann 2014; Huffman and Cohen 2004).

Another reason that women experience lower earnings compared to men is because there is an assumption that women will leave the work force at some point to take care of their families. This is commonly referred to as the "motherhood penalty" (Correll and Benard 2007; Kricheli-Katz 2012). Women are hired at a discount rate to compensate for this loss of time. The first of several problems with this assumption is that many women do not take time off and some do not have families at all, yet they still receive reduced wages. Second, this practice of lower pay is based on circular logic. Women are paid less because they are assumed to be the family member who will take time off from work, thereby making it more likely that they will be the family member who takes time off from work because it would cost more

who frequent brothels, constantly discuss sexual acts, and share pornographic images of women. However, these stories are not simply fiction but dramatizations of real life experiences expressed by servicemen. The military segregates large numbers of post-adolescent men for extended periods of time, and, in wartime, social norms are disrupted and new sexual opportunities and motives emerge resulting in the exploitation of women (Goldstein 2001). Rape is an instrument of domination and has become a tactic to terrorize and humiliate civilians during times of war while self-gratifying the sexual desires of servicemen.

Income Gap

Another manner in which gender inequality presents itself is the gender income or wage gap. In the United States, women earn 79 cents for each dollar that a man earns (DeNavas-Walt and Proctor 2015). That 21% difference in pay has some serious consequences for the quality of life of women and their families (see Poverty section). Obviously, there are laws against wage discrimination

TABLE 6

Median Annual Earnings and Earnings Ratio for Full-time, Year-round Workers, Ages 16 and Older, by State and Gender, 2014

	Men	Women	Earnings Ratio		Men	Women	Earnings Ratio
[1]District of Columbia	$68,932	$61,718	90%	[27]Maine	$45,784	$36,137	79%
[2]New York	$51,580	$44,781	87%	[28]Wisconsin	$47,518	$37,481	79%
[3]Hawaii	$46,786	$40,162	86%	[29]Nebraska	$44,533	$35,101	79%
[4]Maryland	$59,085	$50,481	85%	[30]Texas	$46,235	$36,428	79%
[5]Nevada	$42,294	$35,993	85%	[31]New Mexico	$41,561	$32,473	78%
[6]Florida	$40,971	$34,768	85%	[32]Arkansas	$39,916	$31,161	78%
[7]North Carolina	$41,857	$35,481	85%	[33]Ohio	$47,737	$37,140	78%
[8]California	$50,539	$42,486	84%	[34]Missouri	$45,611	$35,311	77%
[9]Arizona	$43,945	$36,916	84%	[35]Iowa	$47,202	$36,522	77%
[10]Vermont	$46,911	$39,332	84%	[36]Washington	$54,358	$41,926	77%
[11]Connecticut	$61,385	$50,706	83%	[37]Mississippi	$40,850	$31,465	77%
[12]Oregon	$47,194	$38,801	82%	[38]Kansas	$46,951	$36,162	77%
[13]Colorado	$50,898	$41,690	82%	[39]South Dakota	$42,034	$32,048	76%
[14]Massachusetts	$61,611	$50,459	82%	[40]New Hampshire	$55,617	$42,052	76%
[15]Georgia	$44,623	$36,468	82%	[41]Indiana	$46,273	$34,846	75%
[16]Rhode Island	$50,765	$41,469	82%	[42]Michigan	$50,157	$37,419	75%
[17]Tennessee	$41,661	$34,009	82%	[43]Montana	$42,679	$31,696	74%
[18]Minnesota	$51,625	$42,066	81%	[44]Oklahoma	$43,803	$32,186	73%
[19]Delaware	$50,976	$41,278	81%	[45]Idaho	$42,624	$31,019	73%
[20]Alaska	$57,318	$46,288	81%	[46]Alabama	$44,245	$32,136	73%
[21]New Jersey	$60,870	$48,943	80%	[47]North Dakota	$50,624	$36,087	71%
[22]South Carolina	$41,991	$33,719	80%	[48]West Virginia	$45,272	$31,712	70%
[23]Virginia	$52,864	$42,445	80%	[49]Wyoming	$51,926	$35,652	69%
[24]Kentucky	$42,203	$33,704	80%	[50]Utah	$50,937	$34,351	67%
[25]Illinois	$51,652	$40,898	79%	[51]Louisiana	$48,382	$31,586	65%
[26]Pennsylvania	$50,412	$39,905	79%	United States*	$50,383	$39,621	79%

*National data include workers ages 15 and older and are based on data from the U.S. Census Bureau's Current Population Survey.

The Simple Truth about the Gender Pay Gap (Spring 2016). AAUW. Reprinted with the permission of AAUW.

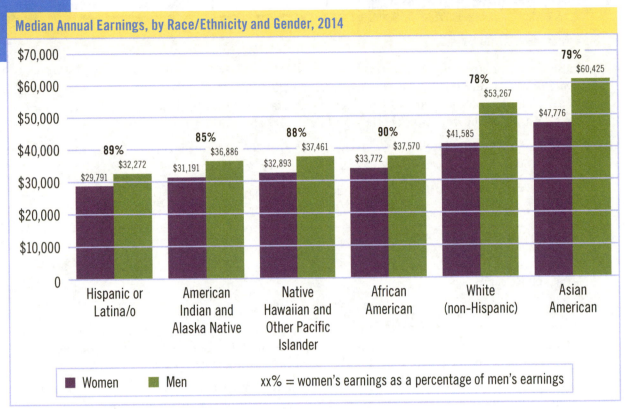

Median Annual Earnings, by Race/Ethnicity and Gender, 2014

Legend: ■ Women ■ Men   xx% = women's earnings as a percentage of men's earnings

Race/Ethnicity	Women	Men	Women's % of Men's
Hispanic or Latina/o	$29,791	$32,272	89%
American Indian and Alaska Native	$31,191	$36,886	85%
Native Hawaiian and Other Pacific Islander	$32,893	$37,461	88%
African American	$33,772	$37,570	90%
White (non-Hispanic)	$41,585	$53,267	78%
Asian American	$47,776	$60,425	79%

Note: Based on median annual earnings of full-time, year-round workers, ages 16 and older

The Simple Truth about the Gender Pay Gap (Spring 2016). AAUW. Reprinted with the permission of AAUW.

for the man to take time off from work. Third, this argument ignores the value of the work that women are doing when they take time off to take care of their families. This is work that benefits society. They are producing and caring for the next generation of workers or taking care of the generation of workers that helped to produce them and give them opportunities. If so many women were not willing to perform this valuable work, who would and how much would it cost?

Strategies to reduce the gender wage gap include: more employer monitoring and reporting of discrepancies, mandating paid family and medical leave, providing increased educational opportunities, and embracing an ideological shift that does not assume that women are less capable than men in any arena.

Social Class

A primary concern of the discipline of sociology is examining the manner in which society is structured, organized, and ordered. The way people are rank ordered or socially stratified determines what their access will be to important resources. Examining this social stratification answers an essential question: Who gets what resources and why? In the United States, an open stratification system presents the possibility of mobility, but the reality is that upward mobility is difficult to achieve. Closed stratification systems are those where mobility is not possible such as a caste system, where your status is determined at birth and fixed for life. For most of the history of the United States, **upward intergenerational mobility**—surpassing the socioeconomic standing of the previous generation—was the expectation. This is why so many immigrants came to and continue to

Persuasive Editorial

Persuasive arguments help people frame their ideas and take position about a topic. Writing a persuasive editorial gives you the opportunity to convince others to agree with the facts you present about an issue that is important to you. Here is an example of an "Op-Ed" column: http://www.nytimes.com/2015/09/07/opinion/charles-m-blow-sexual-attraction-and-fluidity.html?_r=0.

Follow the steps below to develop a persuasive editorial of 500–750 words on a current issue you feel passionate about or are concerned about regarding gender or sexuality.

1. Identify a current issue regarding gender or sexuality:

    a. Income gap

    b. Beyond the gender binary

    c. Rape in the military

    d. Pornography

2. Formulate a position or side of the problem you will argue.

3. Research information presented in the text about the issue you selected and use at least two additional scholarly or peer-reviewed sources that provide evidence to support your position or argument and help you understand the counter argument or opposing position.

4. Write an introduction with a thesis or focus statement that will gain audience attention by including an unusual detail, anecdote, statistic, fact, strong statement, or quotation.

5. Write your narrative or body of your editorial consisting of at least three paragraphs backing your thesis statement with one of the paragraphs addressing counter or opposing arguments.

6. Write a conclusion summarizing your thesis statement, the most important details of your argument, and your call for action.

come to these shores. Recently, the U.S. economy has made it quite challenging to meet this expectation. How people are socially stratified or rank ordered in terms of a class system matters because a person's social class status affects many other aspects of their well-being, such as health, life expectancy, education, political attitudes, gender norms and values, and parenting styles and strategies.

Economic Inequality

Given the significant role that social class plays in determining a person's social well-being in the United States, it is important to examine how economic resources are distributed. Over time, the three broad economic class groups: Upper, Middle, and Lower, expanded to include an upper middle and a lower middle or working class. The gap between the rich and the poor has been growing for some time (Parker 2012) and more people are finding it difficult to maintain their middle-class status (Leigh-Preston 1986), as the number of categories to identify the middle class has increased. Why has the number of categories to identify the middle class increased? The middle is appealing and safe. The ideology of a "classless" society in which Americans are all just "middle class" serves several functions in society: 1) it protects the upper class from negative labels such as greedy and exploitative; 2) it suggests that, if an individual is financially struggling, it is the individual's "fault" and not the economic system and, thus, serves to motivate that individual to work harder to achieve a share of "the American

Dream" of financial security; and 3) it shields the lower class from criticism about being needy and unmotivated. Even though, by definition, one cannot have a "middle" class without an "upper" class and a "lower" class, most people identify themselves as being part of the middle class. Statistically speaking, everyone, not even most people, can be in the "true" middle (average) class. Less frequently mentioned is the expansion at the bottom, which makes room for the **underclass** (Auletta 1982; Wilson 1987)—individuals who experience extremely high rates of poverty and reside in hyper-segregated areas of society.

The numbers show a very uneven distribution of resources in terms of both income and wealth across social class groups that has been growing since 1979. When the economic class groups are broken into quintiles, the top 20% receives almost 50% of the income, while the bottom 20% receives less than 4% of the income. The inequality is even more pronounced when the wealth distribution is highlighted. The top 20% of the population in the United States controls 85% of the wealth, which leaves the bottom 20% in a deficit where they control –1% of the wealth (Wolff 2012).

A simple way to determine how much income inequality exists in a society is to compare the median income to the mean income. In the United States, the mean ($73,738) is considerably higher than the median ($53,657) (DeNavas-Walt and Proctor 2015). This suggests many individuals are earning extremely higher salaries than what the average person earns, thereby pulling the overall mean up, but the median is more indicative of the average person's experience. Other signs of the growing inequality in the United States include the growing gap between the wages of the average employee and the CEO and a continuously rising **Gini Index**. Currently, the average CEO of a Fortune 500 corporation = earns 354 times as much as the average worker in the company (www.afl-cio.org). New policies implemented to require that CEO pay rates are published are not expected to reduce this gap. The Gini index measures inequality on a scale from 0 to 1. When there is no inequality in a society, the Gini score would be 0. If one

WORD BANK ESTIMATES

Click on the link below to view the Gini Index or income distribution by country: http://data.worldbank.org/indicator/SI.POV.GINI

(The World Bank 2016)

person in a society owned all economic resources, this would produce a Gini score of 1, because the society would be completely inequitable (DeNavas-Walt and Proctor 2015). According to The World Bank (2016), the United States has an income distribution of 0.411 on the Gini Index.

How these economic resources are distributed matters because growing inequality calls into question whether social class mobility is a realistic goal for most people. Is the American Dream still achievable? Most Americans hold onto the notion that the "Dream" is alive in the form of a meritocracy, where those who work hard are rewarded and move up in the world (McNamee and Miller 2009). Michael Young, who coined the term *meritocracy* in his 1958 book *The Rise of the Meritocracy*, regrets bringing it into the lexicon, because it does not allow for the consideration of how family resources, professional networks and connections and structural factors such as discrimination determine employment and success outcomes. He is also concerned that suggesting that where a person ends up is due to their merit by default may suggest that when people end up in poverty or a challenging financial position, it is due to their own efforts or lack thereof (Young 2001). In sociology, we call this type of explanation, "blaming the victim" (Ryan 1976).

Poverty

In the 52 years the U.S. Census Bureau has been publishing statistics on poverty, more people were living in poverty in the United States in 2014 than ever before: 46.7 million people or 14.8% of the U.S. population compared to 11.3% in 2000. That is, 1 in 7 Americans live below the official poverty line, which was $23,850 for a family of four in 2014. Yet, this issue seems to be ignored by the mainstream media. For example, in the first five Republican Presidential Primary Debates and the first three Democratic Debates, not one moderator asked a question involving the words "poverty" or "poor." While the topic has been touched upon by some candidates, the topic has been entirely unmentioned by the moderators. A 2015 study in *The Intercept* found poverty's non-status on television is not just limited to the debates. Cable news was over 20 times more likely to mention ISIS or terrorism than poverty during the heart of primary season in late 2015 (Jilani 2015). Yet, which poses a greater threat to the security and prosperity of our country?

Poverty has been linked to diminished IQ in children and poor health (Tucker-Drob and Bates 2018); it impacts childhood education, crime and even future economic gains. A 2011 study attributed 133,000 deaths a year to poverty-related illnesses (Galea, Tracy, Hoggatt, DiMaggio, and Karpati 2011).

Who is poor varies considerably across demographic groups. Children are the age demographic most vulnerable to poverty, with 21.1% of them falling below the poverty line, while the elderly have the lowest rates of poverty across all age groups (10%). African Americans (26.2%) and Hispanic/Latino Americans (23.6%) experience much higher rates of poverty than Asian (12%) and White Americans (10.1%) (DeNavas-Walt and Proctor 2015).

Women (16.1%) are more likely to be poor than men (13.4%). This phenomenon is typically referred to as the **feminization of poverty** (Pearce 1978), but the underlying tone of this term suggests that poverty is something women embrace and choose to take ownership of. Referring to this phenomenon as the **pauperization of women** would be more appropriate, since women and the children in their care are living in poverty at greater rates than men.

Many factors contribute to the higher rates of poverty among women, including increases in female-headed households, increases in the percentage of births that occur outside of marriage, lower rates of marriage and divorce rates

that have declined but stabilized at a high level, lack of access to birth control among poor populations, occupational segregation, and wage discrimination.

Determining who is poor requires deciding whether to use an absolute or relative measure of poverty. A relative measure considers how a person or household compares to the average person or household in the society and, if a person or household falls significantly below the average person or household, then the person/household would be counted as poor. The U.S. government prefers to use an absolute measure, which is based upon how much it would cost to meet a person's or family's minimum or basic needs in terms of items such as food, clothing, and shelter. This figure is then established as the poverty threshold and if a household falls below this level of income, the members of the household are counted as poor. This poverty threshold varies by family size and the ages of the family members. The poverty threshold makes adjustments for inflation each

©Joseph Sohm/ Shutterstock.com

year, but it does not vary based on geographic region and it does not take cost of living changes into consideration.

What is the **poverty threshold** or **poverty line** based upon? The original poverty threshold established in 1963 was just under $3,000 for a typical family of four with two adults and two children. In 2014, the poverty threshold was $23,850 for that same family structure and size. An economist from the Social Security Administration (SSA), Mollie Orshansky, developed the original poverty threshold in 1963. Orshansky based her calculations on the typical middle-income family, which at the time spent about a third of its income on food. Next, she calculated that it would cost about $1,000 to feed the four members of the family three meals a day for a year. Since the families were spending a third of their income on food, the amount it cost to feed the family for one year was multiplied by three and this produced the original poverty threshold which determines who gets counted as poor (Fisher 1992).

There has been and continues to be much debate about whether the poverty threshold is set at an adequate level. Some argue it is too high, but most contend it is too low. Of course, most people who are classified as poor do not fall right below the poverty threshold. Most households or families fall several thousand dollars below the poverty threshold (DeNavas-Walt and Proctor 2015). This is known as the **poverty gap**.

In 1964, President Lyndon Johnson launched a War on Poverty and, over the subsequent decade, the poverty rate fell from 22% to 11%. Is it likely that such a war could be as effective today at reducing the poverty rate? Gans (1995) suggests that there is no motivation to reduce or eliminate poverty in our society because there are too many benefits to having a poor population. As a society, we have too many uses for poor people to really invest in reducing poverty. Gans (1995) identifies five types or categories of uses and thirteen specific uses or functions of poor people for society (see Table 8).

Food Insecurity

In 2014, 14% of all U.S. households reported some form of food insecurity, a decline from a high of 14.9% in 2011. **Food insecurity** "is a household-level economic and social condition of limited or uncertain access to adequate food." The several categories or levels of food security that one might experience including: high, marginal, low, and very low (see Table 9). Households that experienced very low food security have a reduction in food intake and a disruption in their normal eating patterns due to a lack of money and other resources (i.e. appliances to properly store and prepare the foods). Only 5.6% of U.S. households experienced very low food security (Coleman-Jensen, Rabbitt, Gregory, and Singh 2015).

Children experienced food insecurity in 9.4% of U.S. households. Only 1.1% of households with children experienced very low food security, this

TABLE 8				
Types of Uses of the Undeserving Poor				
Microsocial	**Economic**	**Normative**	**Political**	**Macrosocial**
• Risk reduction • Supplying objects of revenge and repulsion	• Creating jobs for better off • Supplying illegal goods • Reserve army of labor	• Moral legitimation • Value reinforcement • Popular culture villains	• Institutional scapegoating • Conservative power shifting • Spatial stigmatization	• Reproduction of stigma and the stigmatized • Forcing the poor out of the labor force

Gans 1995

is because children are usually protected through in-kind assistance programs such as Supplemental Nutrition Assistance Program (SNAP), the Women, Infants, and Children (WIC) program, and the National School Lunch program. Sixty-one percent of food-insecure households reported utilizing these programs in the previous month. Obviously, one of the main factors that contributes to food insecurity is poverty. Households with limited financial resources struggle to provide adequate nutrition to its members (Coleman-Jensen et al. 2015).

Another less discussed factor is the presence of **food deserts**. Poor people are much more likely to live in food deserts. Food deserts are "urban neighborhoods and rural towns without access to fresh, healthy, and affordable food." Such communities may have no food access or food access that is limited to fast food restaurants, convenience stores, and/or small grocery stores. 23.5 million people in the United States live in food deserts. Over 50% of these people are low-income. To be recognized as a food desert, a community must meet two criteria: 1) a poverty rate of at least 20%, and 2) at least 500 persons or 33% of the census tract's population must live more than one mile from a supermarket or large grocery store. The distance is 10 miles for non-metropolitan or rural areas. 2.3 million people live in designated food deserts in rural areas (http://www.ers.usda.gov/amber-waves/2011-december/data-feature-mapping-food-deserts-in-the-us.aspx#.V_A4KE1THIV).

©Crystal Eye Studio/Shutterstock.com

Many health concerns are associated with food insecurity, from the obvious such as hunger and malnutrition to the less obvious such as obesity, which leads to increased risk for many chronic illnesses such as heart disease, diabetes, and cancer. By tracking the food deserts, it has been possible to direct funds and other resources to these areas. Nineteen programs have been established in a joint effort by the U. S. Department of Agriculture (USDA), the Treasury department, and Health and Human Services (HHS) to facilitate the development of grocery stores, small retailers, farmers markets, and corner stores across the United States, with the goal of increasing access to healthy and affordable while eradicating food deserts (http://www.ers.usda.gov/amber-waves/2011-december/data-feature-mapping-food-deserts-in-the-us.aspx#.V_A4KE1THIV). "In 2009, the U.S. Treasury Department's Community Development Financial Institutions (CDFI) Fund, USDA, and HHS created the

TABLE 9

Food Security Categories	
High	No reported indications of food—access problems or limitations.
Marginal	1 or 2 reported indications—typically of anxiety over food sufficiency or shortage of food in the house. Little or no indication of change in diets or food intake.
Low	Reports of reduced quality, variety, or desirability of diet. Little or no indication of reduced food intake.
Very low	Reports of multiple indications of disrupted eating patterns and reduced food intake.

Coleman-Jensen et al. 2015

Inequality is...

Inequality among wages, income, wealth, and opportunity in the United States has increased dramatically over the last 40 years. The Economic Policy Institute has developed an interactive simulation to help people understand how economic policy in the United States has impacted low- and middle-income workers. Click on the link below to find out how economic policy is affecting you.

http://inequality.is/

Explain your thoughts about the simulation activity by addressing the following questions:

1. What was your reaction or feelings about the information you viewed during the simulation?

2. What is the most important idea or concept presented in the simulation?

3. Do you agree or disagree with the economic policy information presented in the simulation activity? Justify your position.

4. Do you think the simulation provided an accurate account of economic policy and the influence it is having on your life? Explain.

■ U.S. FOOD ACCESS AND ENVIRONMENT

Click on the following links to examine the spatial overview of: 1) health food accessibility and 2) food and supermarket accessibility by census tract.

1. Food Environment Atlas: http://www.ers.usda.gov/data-products/food-environment-atlas/go-to-the-atlas.aspx

2. Food Access Research Atlas: http://www.ers.usda.gov/data-products/food-access-research-atlas/go-to-the-atlas.aspx

(USDA 2016)

Healthy Food Financing Initiative (HFFI) to improve access to healthy food in low-income communities" (Association of State and Territorial Health Officials 2014:2). "The 2014 Farm Bill reauthorized the Farmers Market Promotion Program to fund farmer-to-consumer direct marketing projects programs and added the Local Food Promotion Program to include funding for promotion of local and regional food business enterprises that serve as intermediaries to process, distribute, aggregate, and/or store locally or regionally produced food products" (Healthy Food Access Portal).

Evaluating Critical Thinking and Credibility

In this module, we examined how culture influences thinking and behavior. The power of culture resonates within each of us and shapes how we perceive and understand the world. The ability to develop a sociological imagination requires each of us to understand how culture affects our understanding of the world and has the power to substantiate fallacies about individuals, groups, organizations, and the social issues we face in everyday life.

1. Reflect back on the social issues presented in this module.

2. Explain your ethnocentric (cultural bias) and sociocentric (social bias) tendencies about the social issues presented.

3. Describe any fallacies you discovered in your thinking about the issues presented and specify which of your assumptions were challenged.

4. Discuss how the information and data in this module might affect changes in your thinking and open your mind to new alternatives or ideas about the issues presented.

Theoretical Analysis

The theoretical paradigms help us examine and understand the social issues we face in society. Each paradigm provides a lens to develop a holistic picture of how a social issue impacts the social world we live in and the thinking and behavior of individuals in society. In applying the theoretical paradigms to social issues, we must re-visit their focus and level of evaluation and analysis. Use the guideline below to analyze one of the social issues in this module using each theoretical paradigm.

Functionalism is a macrosociological perspective, which examines the social world. This paradigm focuses on understanding the purpose or function of our social structure including the relevance of our social systems, institutions, organizations, and processes and their impact on the issue being examined. Taking into account one of the social issues presented in this module, identify the systems, institutions, organizations, and processes involved and how these structures are integrated and influencing the problem—you are applying a functionalist approach to the issue.

Conflict theory is another macrosociological perspective used to observe the social world. The focus of conflict theory is to investigate competing groups involved in a social issue. This paradigm evaluates and analyzes the conflict between social groups and the resources influencing the power structure between them. Examining the same social issue chosen when applying a functionalist approach, consider which social groups are involved in the problem, what the conflict is about, what resources are involved in the conflict, and who has the power to control the issue—you are applying a conflict theorist approach.

Continuing an examination of the social structure, **feminism** is another macrosociological perspective used to observe the social world. Feminists explore the lives and experiences of women and minority groups involved in a social issue. Consider the social issue you are examining and apply a feminist approach to the issue by analyzing how the problem has impacted women and/or minorities by describing their experiences and how the problem has affected their lives.

To complete a comprehensive analysis of the social world, **environmental theory** provides a macrosociological perspective on the evolution of society. This paradigm considers how a social issue has evolved over time in response to the adaptations and changes made by society. Thinking about the social issue you are exploring, research how the issue has changed over time using an environmental theoretical approach by investigating which policies, laws, social movements, and/or other societal developments have influenced the problem.

Interactionism is a microsociological perspective that evaluates the thinking and behavior of individuals on a particular social issue. This paradigm focuses on identifying the labels, stereotypes, and symbolism associated with an issue. Assessing the social issue you are analyzing in this module, identify the labels, stereotypes, and symbolism defining the problem and how use of these words and images are interpreted by individuals in society and influence their interactions.

Exchange theory is another microsociological perspective used to observe thinking and behavior of individuals in society. Exchange theorists investigate how people are interest driven. Think about the social problem you are studying and pinpoint what is motivating people's involvement or disengagement in the issue. By understanding how people assess and evaluate their role and interests around an issue, you are applying an environmental theorist approach.

Application of each of sociological paradigms helps us examine and understand social issues. They also provide us a method for gathering information from an objective perspective furthering development of our sociological imagination. The theories are useful tools to research social issues and build critical thinking skills.

Social Policy

As people navigate the world in search of their identity and legacy, there are times in their lives when they may feel a need to participate in social action or reform. In some instances, people take action on a small or microsociological scale by helping individuals and families resolve personal problems that in some extent accumulate to impact society at large (i.e., drug issues, health problems, etc.). At other times, people choose to take action on a large or macrosociological scale to address social problems.

A good macrosociological approach in addressing social problems is to alter the way people think and act. Creating awareness or teaching people how to think about something differently or modify behavior is by constructing new rules or norms in which we function or live. When new laws or formal policies are developed and adopted, people are forced to change both thinking and behavior. Take for example, the correlation between texting while driving with the increase of traffic accidents as reported by the U.S. Department of Transportation National Highway Traffic Safety Administration (see http://www.distraction.gov/downloads/pdfs/blueprint-for-ending-distracted-driving.pdf for information and statistics). The most recent approach to reduce the number of fatalities resulting from distracted driving related to cell phone use and texting is to develop new laws throughout the United States banning texting while driving. By creating new laws, people learn and become aware of the dangers associated with texting while driving and are forced to re-think and adjust their behavior while operating a car or vehicle otherwise risk formal punishment if a violation of the law occurs. Because constructing new norms are an effective way to address a social problem and impact the most people, working on creating new policy is a primary intervention used to improve social conditions.

Each year, numerous individuals and groups participate in policy development in an effort to encourage changes in federal, state, and local laws. Consider the cultural issues discussed in this module and generate a list of new policy proposals being deliberated in your community or state or nationally.

1. Identify at least one new policy being proposed to address a social issue related to race, immigration, gender, sexuality, or social class?
2. Who drafted the policy proposal?
3. Who supports the proposal? Who opposes the proposal?
4. Who must approve the proposal to enact a new law?
5. How will approval of the new law change the thinking and behavior of individuals?

Social Movements and Reform

Any discussion about social problems must include a conversation about solutions. Each of the social issues presented in this module have a variety of groups working to change, reform, or address the problem. The success of any social transformation depends on the unity, resources, and persistence of the social group working towards change. Successful social movements require a structure and organization to ensure the group's message is clear, membership is developed, and financial and other resources are garnered to sustain operations.

©a katz/Shutterstock.com

Each of the following groups is working toward social transformation on some of the issues presented in this module to impact policy development.

- #BLACKLIVESMATTER
  (http://blacklivesmatter.com/)
- Human Rights Campaign
  (http://www.hrc.org/)
- Food Recovery Network
  (http://www.foodrecoverynetwork.org/)
- No Kid Hungry
  (https://www.nokidhungry.org/)

Research and investigate these organizations to assess the impact they are having on the social issue they are addressing.

1. What is the mission/goal of the organization?
2. What is the history of the organization? When was it founded?
3. How many members are involved in their organization?
4. What is the process for joining the organization and/or volunteering?
5. What support does the organization receive (e.g., grants, donations, volunteers, etc.)?
6. Who provides financial and other support to the organization?
7. What success in social transformation or changing social policy has the organization demonstrated to date? Explain the group's achievements and/or challenges to success.
8. Identify any groups or movements in your community addressing the social problems presented in this module.

References

ACLU. 2008. "Driving While Black or Brown. An Analysis of Racial Profiling in Arizona." American Civil Liberties Union of Arizona. Retrieved June 12, 2016 (http://www.acluaz.org/sites/default/files/documents/DrivingWhileBlackorBrown.pdf).

Antrosio, Jason. 2012. "Denisovans, Neandertals, Archaics as Human Races." *Living Anthropologically*. Retrieved August 31, 2016 (http://www.livinganthropologically.com/anthropology/denisovans-neandertals-human-races/).

Association of State and Territorial Health Officials. 2014. "Enable Access to Healthy Food Choices." Retrieved June 28, 2016 (http://www.astho.org/Programs/Health-in-All-Policies/Environmental-Health-in-All-Policies/Enable-Access-to-Healthy-Food-Choices/).

Auletta, Ken. 1982. *The Underclass*. New York: Random House.

Bakalian, Anny and Medhi Bozorgmehr. 2009. *Backlash 9/11: Middle Eastern and Muslim Americans Respond*. Berkeley, CA: University of California Press.

Banton, Michael. 1987. *Racial Theories*. Cambridge, MA: Cambridge University Press.

Blidner, Rachelle. 2015. "Elisabeth Hasselbeck suggests Black Lives Matter Movement is Hate Group." *New York Daily News*, September 1. Retrieved June 12, 2016 (http://www.nydailynews.com/news/national/elisabeth-hasselbeck-black-lives-matter-hate-group-article-1.2344132).

Bonilla-Silva, Eduardo. 2009. *Racism without Racists*. Oxford, UK: Rowman & Littlefield Publishers, Inc.

Bourdieu, Pierre. 1991. *Language and Symbolic Power*. Cambridge, MA: Polity Press.

Bridge, Gary. 2006. "Perspectives on Cultural Capital and the Neighbourhood." *Urban Studies*. 43(4):719–730.

Chong, Yee Won. 2012. "Beyond the Gender Binary: Yee Won Chong at TEDxRainier." YouTube. Retrieved October 29, 2015 (https://youtu.be/-Lm4vxZrAig).

Coleman-Jensen, Alisha, Matthew Rabbitt, Christian Gregory, and Anita Singh. 2015. "Household Food Security in the United States in 2014. Washington, D.C.: U.S. Department of Agriculture, Economic Research Report Number 194, September. Retrieved June 12, 2016 (http://www.ers.usda.gov/media/1896841/err194.pdf).

Collins, Patricia Hill. 1993. "Toward a New Vision: Race, Class, and Gender as Categories of Analysis and Connection." *Race, Sex, & Class* 1(1):25–45.

Collins, Patricia Hill. 2009. *Another Kind of Public Education.* Boston, MA: Beacon Press.

Correll, Shelley J. and Stephen Benard. 2007. "Getting a Job: Is There a Motherhood Penalty?" *American Journal of Sociology* 112(5):1297–1339.

Cose, Ellis. 1993. *The Rage of a Privileged Class: Why Are Middle-Class Blacks Angry? Why Should America Care?* New York: HarperCollins Publishers, Inc.

"Deadly Attacks Since 9/11." 2016. New America. Retrieved June 1, 2016 (http://securitydata.newamerica.net/extremists/deadly-attacks.html).

DeNavas-Walt, Carmen and Bernadette D. Proctor. 2015. "Current Population Reports, Income and Poverty in the United States: 2014." U.S. Census Bureau, Washington, D.C.

Department of Defense. 2012. *Department of Defense Annual Report on Sexual Assault in the Military.* Vol. 1. Washington, D.C.: Department of Defense Sexual Assault Prevention and Response.

D'Souza, Dinesh. [1995] 1996. *The End of Racism: Principles for a Multiracial Society.* Free Press.

Feagin, Joe R. and Melvin P. Sikes. 1994. *Living with Racism: The Black Middle-Class Experience.* Boston, MA: Beacon Press.

Fisher, Gordon M. 1992. "The Development and History of the Poverty Thresholds." *The Social Security Bulletin* 55(4):3.

Galea, Sandro, Melissa Tracy, Katherine J. Hoggatt, Charles DiMaggio, Adam Karpati. 2011. "Estimated Deaths Attributable to Social Factors in the United States." *American Journal of Public Health* 101(8):1456–1465.

Gans, Herbert J. 1995. *The War against the Poor: The Underclass and Antipoverty Policy.* New York: Basic Books.

Goldstein, Joshua S. 2001. *War and Gender: How Gender Shapes the War System and Vice Versa.* New York: Cambridge University Press.

Goleman, Daniel. 1988. "Chemistry of Sexual Desire Yields Its Elusive Secrets." *The New York Times*, October 18. Retrieved June 17, 2016 (http://www.nytimes.com/1988/10/18/science/chemistry-of-sexual-desire-yields-its-elusive-secrets.html?pagewanted=all).

Harris, David. 1999. "Driving While Black: Racial Profiling on Our Nation's Highways." ACLU Special Report. Retrieved June 12, 2016 (https://www.aclu.org/report/driving-while-black-racial-profiling-our-nations-highways).

Hawks, John. 2016. "Earlier Mixture from Modern Humans into Neandertal Populations." Retrieved August 31, 2016 (http://johnhawks.net/weblog/reviews/neandertals/neandertal_dna/neandertal-early-modern-gene-flow-kuhl-wilm-2016.html).

Healthy Food Access Portal. n.d. "Healthy Food Financing Initiative: Federal Government." Retrieved June 28, 2016 (http://healthyfoodaccess.org/findmoney/hffi/federal).

Hegewisch, Ariane and Heidi Hartmann. 2014. "Occupational Segregation and the Gender Wage Gap: A Job Half Done." Institute for Women's Policy Research Briefing Paper IWPR (C 419).

Hensch, Mark. 2015. "Christie's warning to Black Lives Matter: 'Don't call me for a meeting.'" TheHill.com, November 11. Retrieved June 12, 2016 (http://thehill.com/blogs/ballot-box/presidential-races/259898-christie-to-black-lives-matter-dont-call-me-for-a-meeting).

Huffman, Matt L. and Philip N. Cohen. 2004. "Racial Wage Inequality: Job Segregation and Devaluation across U.S. Labor Markets." *American Journal of Sociology* 109(4):902–936.

Hurh, Won Moo and Kwang Chung Kim. 1983. *Korean Immigrants in America: A Structural Analysis of Ethnic Confinement and Adhesive Adaptation*. Madison, NJ: Fairleigh Dickinson University Press.

Jendian, Matthew Ari. 2008. *Becoming American, Remaining Ethnic: The Case of Armenian-Americans in Central California*. New York: LFB Scholarly Publishing.

Jilani, Zaid. 2015. "Obama is Right: Terrorism has taken over Cable News." *The Intercept*. Retrieved June 12, 2016 (https://theintercept.com/2015/12/21/obama-is-right-terrorism-has-taken-over-cable-news/).

Kricheli-Katz, Tamar. 2012. "Choice, Discrimination, and the Motherhood Penalty." *Law & Society Review* 46(3):557–587.

Leigh-Preston, Nancey. 1986. "The Debate Over the Disappearing Middle." *Berkeley Planning Journal* 3(1):119–144. Retrieved June 12, 2016 (http://escholarship.org/uc/item/5362f97g).

Machery, Edouard and Luc Faucher. 2005. "Social Construction and the Concept of Race." *Philosophy of Science* 72(5):1208–1219.

Martin, Philip. 2013. "Immigration and Farm Labor: Policy Options and Consequences." *American Journal of Agricultural Economics* 95(2):470–475.

Massey, Douglas S. 1995. "The New Immigration and Ethnicity in the United States." *Population and Development Review* 21(3):631–652.

McNamee, Stephen J. and Robert K. Miller. 2009. *The Meritocracy Myth*. New York: Rowman & Littlefield, 2009.

Milburn, Michael A., Roxanne Mather, and Sheree D. Conrad. 2000. "The Effects of Viewing R-rated Movie Scenes that Objectify Women on Perceptions of Date Rape." *Sex Roles* 43(9/10):645–664.

Mooney, Chris. 2014. "The Science of Why Cops Shoot Young Black Men and How to Reform our Bigoted Brains." *Mother Jones*. Retrieved June 12, 2016 (http://www.motherjones.com/politics/2014/11/science-of-racism-prejudice).

Nielson, Kate. 2015. "2015 State Equal Pay Legislation by the Numbers." American Association of University Women. Retrieved June 12, 2016 (http://www.aauw.org/2015/08/20/equal-pay-by-state/).

"Nine Healthy Ways to Communicate." 2009. StirFry Seminars and Consulting. Retrieved June 12, 2016 (www.stirfryseminars.com).

Norton, Arron T. and Gregory M. Herek. 2012. "Heterosexuals' Attitudes Toward Transgender People: Findings from A National Probability Sample of U.S. Adults." *Sex Roles* 68(11–12):738–753.

Omi, Michael J. and Howard Winant. 1994. *Racial Formation in the United States: From the 1960s to the 1990s*. Revised edition. New York: Routledge.

Parker, Kim. 2012. "Yes, the Rich Are Different." Pew Research Center. Washington, D.C. Retrieved June 12, 2016 (www.pewsocialtrends.org/2012/08/27/yes-the-rich-are-different/#rich-richer).

Passel, Jeffrey S. and D'vera Cohn. 2015. "Unauthorized Immigrant Population Stable for Half a Decade." Pew Research Center. Washington, D.C. Retrieved June 12, 2016 (http://www.pewresearch.org/fact-tank/2015/07/22/unauthorized-immigrant-population-stable-for-half-a-decade/).

Reay, Diane. 2004. "Education and Cultural Capital: The Implications of Changing Trends in Education Policies." *Cultural Trends* 13(2):73–86.

Robbins, Derek. 2005. "The Origins, Early Development and Status of Bourdieu's Concept of 'Cultural Capital.'" *The British Journal of Sociology* 56(1):13–30.

Ryan, William. 1976. *Blaming the Victim* (Revised Edition). New York: Vintage Books.

Sabina, Chiara, Janis Wolak, and David Finkelhor. 2008. "The Nature and Dynamics of Internet Pornography Exposure for Youth." *Cyberpsychology & Behavior* 11(6):691–693.

Shim, Jae Woong and Bryant Paul. 2014. "The Role of Anonymity in the Effects of Inadvertent Exposure to Online Pornography among Young Adult Males." *Social Behavior and Personality* 42(5):823–834.

Shim, Jae Woong, Seungwhan Lee, and Bryant Paul. 2007. "Who Responds to Unsolicited Sexually Explicit Materials on the Internet? The Role of Individual Differences." *Cyberpsychology & Behavior* 10(1):71–79.

Stack, Steven, Ira Wasserman, and Roger Kern. 2004. "Adult Social Bonds and Use of Internet Pornography." *Social Science Quarterly* 85(1):75–88.

Takaki, Ronald. 2012. *A Different Mirror: A History of Multicultural America* (Revised Edition). eBookIt.com.

"Ten Myths about Immigration." [2011] 2015. Tolerance.org. Retrieved June 12, 2016 (http://www.tolerance.org/immigration-myths; http://www.tolerance.org/article/sources-ten-myths-about-immigration).

The World Bank. 2016. "Gini Index (World Bank Estimate)." Retrieved June 27, 2016 (http://data.worldbank.org/indicator/SI.POV.GINI).

Tuch, Steven A. and Ronald Weitzer. 1999. "The Polls—Trends: Racial Differences in Attitudes Toward the Police." *Public Opinion Quarterly* 61:642–663.

Tucker-Drob, Elliot M. and Timothy C. Bates. 2016. "Large Cross-National Differences in Gene × Socioeconomic Status Interaction on Intelligence." *Psychological Science* 27(2):138–149. Retrieved June 12, 2016 (http://pss.sagepub.com/content/27/2/138).

USDA. 2016. "Food Access." Retrieved June 27, 2016 (http://www.ers.usda.gov/topics/food-choices-health/food-access.aspx).

Waller Meyers, Deborah. 2006. "From Horseback to High-Tech: U.S. Border Enforcement." Migration Policy Institute. Washington, D.C. Retrieved June 12, 2016 (http://www.migrationpolicy.org/article/horseback-high-tech-us-border-enforcement).

Wang, Wendy, Kim Parker, and Paul Taylor. 2013. "Breadwinner Moms: Mothers are the Sole or Primary Provider in Four-in-Ten Households with Children; Public Conflicted about the Growing Trend." Pew Research Center. Washington, D.C. Retrieved June 12, 2016 (http://www.pewsocialtrends.org/2013/05/29/breadwinner-moms).

Warren, Patricia, Donald Tomaskovic-Devey, William Smith, Matthew Zingraff, and Marcinda Mason. 2006. "Driving While Black: Bias Processes and Racial Disparity in Police Stops." *Criminology* 44(3):709–738.

Weitzer, Ronald. 1999. "Citizens' Perceptions of Police Misconduct: Race and Neighborhood Context." *Justice Quarterly* 16(4): 819–846.

Weitzer, Ronald. 2000. "Racialized Policing." *Law and Society Review* 34(1):129–155.

Weitzer, Ronald and Steven A. Tuch. 1999. "Race, Class, and Perception of Discrimination by the Police." *Crime & Delinquency* 45(4):494–507.

Weitzer, Ronald and Steven A. Tuch. 2002. "Perceptions of Racial Profiling: Race, Class, and Personal Experience." *Criminology* 40:435–456.

Wilson, William Julius. 1987. *The Truly Disadvantaged: The Inner City, The Underclass and Public Policy.* Chicago, IL: University of Chicago Press.

Wilson, Meagan Meuchel. 2014. *Hate Crime Victimization, 2004–2012—Statistical Tables.* Bureau of Justice Statistics. NCJ 244409. Washington, D.C.: U.S. Department of Justice.

Wise, Tim. 2005. *White Like Me: Reflections on Race from a Privileged Son.* Brooklyn, NY: Soft Skull Press.

Wolff, Edward N. 2012. *The Asset Price Meltdown and the Wealth of the Middle Class.* New York: New York University.

Ybarra, Michele L. and Kimberly J. Mitchell. 2005. "Exposure to Internet Pornography among Children and Adolescents: A National Survey." *Cyberpsychology & Behavior* 8(5):473–486.

Yinger, J. Milton. 1994. *Ethnicity: Source of Strength? Source of Conflict?* Albany, NY: State University of New York Press.

Young, Michael. 2001. "Down with Meritocracy." *The Guardian*, June 29. Retrieved June 12, 2016 (http://www.theguardian.com/politics/2001/jun/29/comment).

Zillmann, Dolf and Jennings Bryant. 1984. "Effects of Massive Exposure to Pornography." Pp. 115–138 in *Pornography and sexual aggression* by Neil M. Malamuth & Edward Donnerstein. Orlando, FL: Academic Press.

Do you know the terms?

Using the list provided below, create a personal dictionary of key terms and concepts presented in this module. Include the term, phonetic spelling (if needed), and definition in your own words. Next, provide a real world example of the term or concept based on your previous knowledge or new information you learned in this module to help re-enforce learning.

Cisgender
Color-blind racism
Conflict theory
Cultural capital
Cultural diffusion
Cultural lag
Cultural leveling
Cultural relativism
Cultural universals
Culture
Economic inequality
Environmental theory
Ethnocentrism
Exchange theory
Feminism
Feminization of poverty
Food deserts
Food insecurity
Functionalism
Gender
Gini index
Ideal culture

Immigration
Imperialism
Income gap
Material culture
Non-material culture
Pauperization of women
Pornography
Poverty gap
Poverty threshold
Race
Racial profiling
Rape in the military
Real culture
Sex
Sexual orientation
Social class
Symbolic interactionism
Transgender
Underclass
Upward intergenerational mobility
White privilege

MODULE 4

Political Economy

Political Ideology and Economic Theory

In every country throughout the world, politics and money are associated with governance and the fight for power to control economic, legal, and social decisions. Social groups develop **political parties** and factions to gain power in governments and influence policies as a way to exert control. Political parties maintain ideological principles and standards they believe as the design for social order. People in politics think their prevailing issues are righteous and set the course for how governance should be propagated in a country or region. In the fight for power and control, political parties and factions have competing interests and find methods to obtain and wield power over people, either voluntarily (e.g., social movements, elections, and incentives) or by force (e.g., war, violence, and intimidation).

Power is closely associated with money in politics and is defined by the sociologist Max Weber ([1921, 1925:28] 2013) as "the ability of an individual or group to achieve their own goals or aims when others are trying to prevent them from realizing them." Governing bodies and political organizations ideologically work to influence the economy of a nation or territory. The wealth and resources of a country are a direct result of its production, distribution, and accumulation of goods and services. Power over a country's **economy** influences its fiscal and monetary policies surrounding productivity, employment, inflation, interest rates, market trends, consumer confidence, exchange rates, stock market activity, and taxes.

Many people support the **economic theory** of John Maynard Keynes (1936) and view an increasing consumption of goods as economically beneficial. This perspective compliments capitalism or a privately-held system for profit where the goals

©NLshop/Shutterstock.com

©Sergei Bachlakov/Shutterstock.com

of production focus on sales for financial growth. This philosophical approach focuses on consumer spending with the assumption that profits will be re-invested into the market and communities, leading to economic prosperity for all. The theory relies on re-investing profits, but power and greed interfere with social responsibility. Even Keynes realized individuals are unable to promote the general interest above egocentric interest and most capitalists worsen the situation by keeping profits to themselves rather than re-investing and sharing them (Carabelli and Cedrini 2013).

Social Issues

Domination and Hegemony

Western society emphasizes the importance of pluralism and freedom, but within that framework some groups are able to maintain a dominant identity. This is similar to the scenario in George Orwell's *Animal Farm* (1946:123), where "all animals are equal, but some animals are more equal than others." Whether it is the dominant sex, race, class, sexual orientation, language, or country, stated and unstated benefits exist for the dominant group. In contrast, those who find themselves outside of the dominant group frequently struggle to find acceptance or even tolerance.

At a global level, recall that **World Systems Theory** divides countries into three categories: core, semi-periphery, and periphery. Core countries dominate the geopolitical landscape, which allows them to dictate how resources are distributed. Core countries are able to create global political and economic policies that allow them to remain at the center of world markets. Rich countries become richer, while poor countries struggle to remain afloat. The end result is a **hegemonic** world that perpetuates the ethnocentric attitudes and behaviors that allow the core countries and their elite groups to maintain their dominance.

Campaign Finance

The influence of money in political campaigns has long been a subject of concern in American democracy. **Political Action Committees** (PACS) are special interest groups with a specific goal of raising and spending funds to support and defeat candidates for political offices. PACS have strict limits on how much they are allowed to donate to any one candidate or political party. PACS can contribute up to $5,000 to a candidate's committee per election, $15,000 to any one national political party annually, and up to $5,000 annually to any other PAC. PACS are allowed to receive up to $5,000 each year from any person, PAC, or party committee. In January 2010, the U.S. Supreme Court's 5–4 decision in *Citizens United v. Federal Election Commission* declared that political spending is protected under the First Amendment (i.e., freedom of speech), so corporations and unions could now spend unlimited amounts of money on political activities, as long as it was done independently of a party or candidate. Then, in 2014, the U.S. Supreme Court's 5–4 ruling in *McCutcheon v. Federal Election Commission* abolished limits on the total amount any individual can give directly to federal candidates, party committees, and affiliated political committees in any election cycle. These two decisions have opened the floodgates of financial contributions political campaigns and resulted in greater control of electoral outcomes in the United States by the elite. Super PACS do not contribute funds to candidates or political parties, but rather spend money in federal races on ads and mail to influence voters to elect or defeat certain candidates. Unlike PACS, super PACS have no limits on how much they can spend. In comparison, individual citizens are allowed to contribute up to $2,000 per candidate in each election (http://www.fec.gov/info/contriblimitschart1516.pdf). In the 2016 U. S. presidential campaign season, by June 2016 over $827 million dollars had been raised by the candidates (FEC 2016b).

FIGURE 14

2014 PAC Summary Data	
Select a Cycle	
Total Receipts	$2,573,872
Total Spent	$2,905,964
Begin Cash on Hand	$873,822
End Cash on Hand	$541,729
Debts	$0
Independent Expenditures	$988,038
Date of last report	December 31, 2014

2014 PAC Contribution Data	
Contributions from *this PAC to federal candidates* (list recipients) (0% to Democrats, 100% to Republicans)	$453,000
Contributions to *this PAC from individual donors of $200 or more* (list donors)	$192,681

Many citizens and organizations are concerned that the presence of so much money in the elections allows the donors to influence the decision-making of elected officials. Many watchdog organizations, including the National Institute on Money in State Politics, the Center for Responsive Politics, The Campaign Legal Center, Democracy21, and ProPublica, monitor campaign contributions and the voting records of the elected officials who receive them. Several attempts to reform the campaign finance system have been made. In 2002, a bipartisan bill sponsored by Senators McCain and Feingold passed. The bill focused upon eliminating "soft" money or money contributed to a political party or organization to be spent in any manner determined necessary during the election process. Several revisions were made to the original proposal and ultimately what passed was considered a much weaker version of the original legislation (FEC 2016a). This effort to contain the influence of big donations was easily circumvented with the advent of the super PAC following the *Citizens United* decision. Some political leaders continue to call for campaign finance reform. One 2016 presidential candidate, Bernie Sanders, made campaign finance reform a central theme in his run for office, and nationally, **Move to Amend**—"a coalition of hundreds of organizations and hundreds of thousands of individuals committed to social and economic justice, ending corporate rule, and building a vibrant democracy that is genuinely accountable to the people, not corporate interests"—formed in September 2009. Move to Amend is calling for a 28th Amendment to *The U.S. Constitution* that would "unequivocally state that inalienable rights belong to human beings only and that money is not a form of protected free speech under the First Amendment and can be regulated in political campaigns" (see http://vimeo.com/93687066 for sample text in video format). On September 11, 2014, a majority of the U.S. Senate voted 54–42 along party lines to support "The Democracy for All" Amendment (S.J. Res. 19) to re-establish the authority of

Congress and the states to regulate and limit campaign spending. Unfortunately, advancing a constitutional amendment requires a two-thirds vote.

A July 2014 public opinion poll shows, however, that more than three in five voters are opposed to the U.S. Supreme Court's ruling in *Citizens United* and that opposition occurs across party lines, with 61% of Democrats, 62% of Independents, and 58% of Republicans opposed. Even more impressive is the strongly unfavorable impression voters have of special interest and lobbyist spending on elections: "More than three-quarters (76%) hold an unfavorable view towards this spending...[including] 76% of Democrats, 74% of Independents, and 79% of Republicans" (Lake Research Partners and Chesapeake Beach Consulting 2014).

Currently, the candidate with the most money usually wins the election (Montanaro, Wellford, and Pathe 2014). Does this mean that voters are for sale? At the very least, it suggests that voters are easily influenced, and, perhaps, manipulated. A candidate with full coffers, has the luxury of spending liberally on ads (TV, print, Internet, and radio) to persuade voters to support him or her. The more often a person sees or hears from a candidate the more familiar they become with the candidate and this increases his or her chances of voting for that candidate.

One strategy citizens can employ to mitigate the influence of "big money" in the election process is to agree to donate tax dollars to the public campaign fund and then subsequently demand that candidates accept pubic campaign funds, which will automatically limit how much private donor money they can use. Currently, most candidates decline the public campaign funds, because unless each candidate agrees to accept these funds, the candidate who accepts the public funds would be at a tremendous disadvantage. If voters refuse to vote for candidates who do not accept the public funds, then the candidates will be forced to accept the public funds.

Corporate Welfare

Governments provide subsidies or financial aid and support to wealthy corporations at the expense of states, communities, individuals, and unsubsidized corporate taxpayers. Subsidies paid by the government are known as corporate welfare. By definition **corporate welfare** is "any action by local, state or federal government that gives a corporation or an entire industry a benefit not offered to others" (Barlett and Steele 1998:36). Benefits are either in the form of cash payment or tax reduction.

Traditionally, corporate welfare is labeled or referred to in terms of "economic development" or "public-private partnerships" by governments and corporations (Barlett and Steele 1998). Since 2000, the federal government has granted $68 billion in subsidies and special tax credits to 582 large companies in industries such as oil, energy, finance, and defense (New American 2015). The U.S. government justifies corporate welfare as a method for creating jobs and keeping corporations from relocating abroad.

The sad truth is that many local, regional, and state governments pay corporations to create and provide jobs in their communities, but the money granted does not frequently match the investment made. Research on corporate welfare finds benefits are rarely successful in attracting high-skilled, high-paying jobs and the incentives corporations receive aid in destroying competition, distort

©totallypic/Shutterstock.com

labor markets, and inflict long-term damage on the economy (McMahon 2014). Corporate welfare creates economic advantages for the wealthiest corporations and typically does not result in significant job creation. In a 2013 report released by Think by Numbers, massive subsidies offered by the Federal government to industries such as coal, wind, ethanol, and oil constitute a significant portion of corporate welfare (see http://thinkbynumbers.org/government-spending/corporate-welfare/corporate-vs-social-welfare/). The amount spent on corporate welfare exceeds the amount spent on the nation's poor (Bartlett and Steele 1998).

Government officials do a good job selling the public on economic incentives for corporations. Politicians provide corporate subsidies without having the knowledge or expertise in the industry to understand its viability or impact on the community. Communities are told corporations will provide jobs and increase local revenue. People believe they will have better job opportunities with increased wages. However, corporate subsidies tend to redistribute jobs from one community to another, not create new ones (McMahon 2014). Additionally, once subsidies are depleted and profit margins fall, corporations abandon the infrastructure developed and move to new locations or projects.

Bartlett and Steele (1998) believe the real blame for corporate welfare rests on the politicians who want the perception of improving the economic development of their communities. Yet, corporate subsidies are provided without any explicit agreement to the numbers and quality of jobs created or environmental impact of operations, so there is no accountability by the corporate entity for the taxpayer dollars provided (Murray 2003). Match this with corporations motivated by money to pursue every dollar, and the result is government officials using taxpayer dollars to reward the powerful without any long-term, sustainable commitment to communities and taxpayers.

War Profiteers

War profiteers or military contractors seek profit from warfare. Individuals and groups sell weapons, services, and goods to countries and entities at war to make money. **War profiteers** include arms dealers, mercenaries, research groups, and companies selling commodities or resources for war. These government contractors benefit from the suffering of others who question their moral responsibility as a consequence of what ensues with the weapons, services, and goods they provide.

In 2012, the U.S. Pentagon (in Greenwald and Crowe 2012) reported the quarterly profits of their top three military contractors:

1. Boeing ($923 million)
2. Lockheed Martin ($668 million)
3. Northrop Grumman ($506 million)

U.S. President Abraham Lincoln viewed war profiteering as an immoral and fraudulent exploitation against the U.S. government and taxpayers, which led to the passage of the *False Claims Act* or "Lincoln's Law" in 1863. Nearly 80 years later, U.S. President Franklin D. Roosevelt (1940) stated, "I don't want to see a single war millionaire created in the United States as a result of this world disaster." President Roosevelt relentlessly investigated and exposed war profiteers during his presidency. During the 21st century, the U.S. House of Representatives introduced the War Profiteering Prevention Act of 2007 (https://www.govtrack.us/congress/bills/110/hr400/text) to "prohibit profiteering and fraud relating to military action,

©Peter R Foster IDMA/Shutterstock.com

relief, and reconstruction efforts, and for other purposes." Unfortunately, the bill never passed the U.S. Senate. During this time, both Lockheed Martin and Boeing allegedly violated the *False Claims Act* by price-fixing and double-billing resulting in a $20 million settlement in the first quarter of 2012 to halt lawsuits initiated by the U.S. government (Greenwald and Crowe 2012). According to the Department of Justice, Lockheed Martin agreed to pay $27.5 million in 2014 for alleged overbilling (https://www.justice.gov/opa/pr/defense-contractor-agrees-pay-275-million-settle-overbilling-allegations) and $5 million in 2016 to settle allegations for submitting false claims (https://www.justice.gov/opa/pr/lockheed-martin-agrees-pay-5-million-settle-alleged-violations-false-claims-act-and-resource).

Groups and companies profiting from conflict sometimes lead to the development of useful artifacts, devices, or services for society. For example the iPhone Help feature, SIRI, was originally developed by SRI International through U.S. Department of Defense sponsored research at $150 million (Roush 2010). The company generated additional profit from commercializing their work. Many technological advances (i.e., computers, GPS systems, Internet, artificial intelligence, etc.) are a result of military research. Nonetheless, such advances bring into question the ethics of earning profit from war. Both directly and indirectly, war profiteers, including those involved in research, are taking money and benefiting from people being seriously injured or dying.

Despite the controversy of war profiteering, the U.S. government continues to pay millions of dollars to huge corporations each year, even during peacetime. In 2007, Robert Greenwald, film director of the documentary *Iraq for Sale: The War Profiteers*, was invited to testify before Congress, but House Republicans would not allow him to show four minutes from the documentary (see banned excerpts at: https://youtu.be/tVEJq7-GggQ). Sadly, more than $5 million in campaign donations and $33 million in lobbying Congress comes from military contractors (Greenwald and Crowe 2012). Even with the decline in U.S. conflicts abroad, defense contractors look overseas

to make up for slowing sales in the United States (Weigley 2013). Many contractors have profited immensely from the U.S. government, which has the largest military budget in the world.

Media Control

Traditional agents of socialization include the family, the church, schools, and peers, but in the current information age that we find ourselves in another major agent of socialization is the media. What people know, how they think and behave is heavily influenced by what they are exposed to by various forms of media. Between television, radio, newspapers and magazines, social media sites and the Internet in general, information is readily accessible, perhaps too accessible, resulting in information overload. With access to so much information it is challenging to determine what is credible. The irony, however, is that although information seems to be ubiquitous, there is not much variety in the information that people are able to access. This is because just a handful of corporations (Newscorp, Viacom, Disney, CBS, TimeWarner, and Comcast), control the majority of media outlets in the United States (Freepress.net 2016). Although, it seems that there are many options and many channels to choose from, most of these options or alternatives are being managed by the same parent company and the same executives. This allows them to influence the flow of information to the public. Having the ability to control or influence what the public thinks is crucial to the maintenance of the "power elite."

©Stuart Miles/Shutterstock.com

FIGURE 15   AMERICA AS A SUPERPOWER

The world's largest defense budget ($bn)

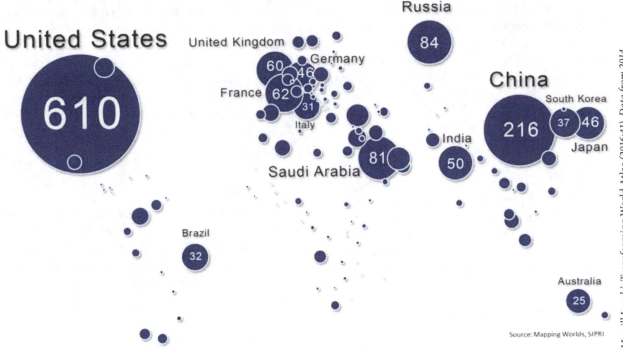

Source: Bank of America Merrill Lynch's Transforming World Atlas (2016:41). Data from 2014.

Source: Mapping Worlds, SIPRI

- The US spends more on its defense budget than the next 15 countries combined
- The US Pentagon spends more than is spent on health, education. welfare, and safety by all 50 US states combined
- In fact, the US has 5% of the world's population, but almost 50% of the world's total military expenditure
- Military spending and technological superiority make the US the sole global superpower, providing geopolitical clout and expectations as to the role as global policeman

In *Media Control*, Noam Chomsky (2002), describes the theory of well-known journalist Walter Lippmann who suggests that the world in divided into two groups the "specialized class," which is a much smaller group, that makes decisions, performs executive functions , and does the thinking and the planning for the entire society and the "bewildered herd" who operate as the "spectators." The bewildered herd or the "masses" must be controlled, tamed, or distracted to keep them from impeding the goals and plans of the specialized or powerful class. The chief tool used to control the masses is media.

The executives, who control the corporations that manage the "information diet" of the public, have billions of dollars at their disposal for advertising. Consumption patterns are heavily influenced by the images that are portrayed in the media. The foods we eat, the cars we drive, even the medicines we take are first introduced to us through advertisements. We may not produce much anymore, now that we have outsourced most of our manufacturing jobs, but we are still a consumer-driven society. Consumption is a natural activity, but the advertising culture in the United States encourages the public to go beyond meeting their needs to fulfill their desires. Advertisements frequently encourage people to purchase items that they never knew existed and never imagined needing. This extreme level of consumption is referred to as consumerism. Like habitual overeating, consumerism is associated with some unhealthy outcomes such as the waste of natural resources, high levels of pollution, overcrowded landfills, the accumulation of debt, working excessive hours to pay for all of the things that you desire, perhaps even legal troubles from breaking the rules to get what you want. This pattern of overconsumption comes at the expense of many developing countries (Robbins 2007) as the United States uses more than its fair share of the world's natural resources and frequently "borrows" the natural resources of low income countries.

Place and Space

Culture has long played a role in geographic development. Investments into community infrastructure and growth have historically been tied to the politics of race, ethnicity, gender, sexuality, and social class. The uneven development of communities results in different spatial patterns of economy, equity, and opportunity in places where people live.

The **political economy of place** has long implications to the people who occupy its space. What a place has to offer its residents affects their level of consciousness, sense of belonging, social will and reproduction, and formation of class and political cultures (Marx 1859). The social production of space is a platform for cultural, political, and economic dominance by groups with existing wealth and resources to control spatial patterns of development and investment with access to public and private funding.

The same holds true for combating or warding off dangers to a community. For example, environmental degradation by nuclear testing in the Southwest region of the United States during the 20th century tells a story of economic and racial inequality towards Native American people living in the area (Konradi and Schmidt 2004). Environmental maps show nuclear test and waste disposal sites were not planned for geographic fit, but rather for the lack of political and economic strength of its residents to resist its implementation.

Climate Change

One of the major controversies in environmental politics has been the labeling of climate change. Scientists originally referred to climate change as global warming to describe the increasing temperature of the earth's atmosphere as a result of increased pollutants. Politicians and citizens interpreted the literal meaning of the label and expected global warming to equate warmer temperatures. When severe weather conditions occur, including snow blizzards, heavy rain, and freezing temperatures, skeptics feel justified in calling global warming a hoax or myth and relinquish any personal responsibility to reducing environmental pollutants.

This confusion and misuse of the label has led scientists to reframe their discussions using the term **climate change** to explain how pollutants affect the environment to increase changes in the

©vasakkohaline/Shutterstock.com

©Piyaset/Shutterstock.com

earth's atmosphere, resulting in extreme weather patterns and deterioration of natural resources and life. A 2016 study, *The Effect of Information Provision on Public Consensus about Climate Change*, examined whether providing scientific evidence on the occurrence and causes of climate change would affect people's own beliefs about the issue (Deryugina and Shurchkov 2016). Results showed people given concrete scientific information were more likely to report believing climate change was real and occurring. However, changes in beliefs about the existence of climate change did not lead people to support policy action or financial contributions to combating climate change.

According to The Intergovernmental Panel on Climate Change, research indicates the net damage cost of climate change is significant and will increase over time (Shaftel 2016). As reported by the Earth Science Commissions Team at NASA's Jet Propulsion Laboratory at California Institute of Technology (in Shaftel 2016), some observable effects of climate change include the shrinking of glaciers, shifting of plants and animal ranges, earlier flowering of trees, loss of sea life, accelerated sea level rise, and intense heat waves. In July 2016, NASA deployed a DC-8 flying laboratory on a 26-day Atmospheric Tomography mission around the globe to measure over 200 gases and airborne particles and understand how much of the Earth's atmospheric chemistry is "normal" and how much is influenced by pollution sources.

Biodiversity

Biodiversity refers to the variability of living organisms at genetic, species, and ecosystem levels (MEA 2005). Climate change, land use, and privatization of natural resources are the biggest threats to biodiversity conservation. The 21st century lifestyle of urbanization and technology are leaving a direct footprint on the planet and displacing species (Kreitler, Schloss, Soong, Hannah, and Davis 2015). Our modern-day, industrial practices have a negative impact on plant and animal populations and their natural communities. The net result is a loss of life and diverse populations, affecting the ecological balance of the planet and the well-being of the human species.

Over the last century, the extinction of 100 birds, mammals, and amphibians has been documented (MEA 2005:3–4). Biodiversity has declined substantially throughout the globe, compromising interdependency of different species. The Millennium Ecosystem Assessment (2005) found a decline in population size and range for the majority of species across all taxonomic groups inhabiting the earth.

Sociological Application 4.1

U.S. Climate Change

Visit the **National Climate Assessment** website:
http://nca2014.globalchange.gov/

1. Explore *Full Report* on the right-hand side of the screen.

2. Select *Sectors* then click *Explore Sectors*.

3. Choose a sector to learn about.

4. Read and evaluate the information and graphs presented about the impact of climate change on the sector you chose.

5. Prepare a summary discussing how climate change is impacting the sector you reviewed.

6. Develop three realistic solutions to address the impact climate change is having on the sector you studied.

©Dirk Ercken/Shutterstock.com

BIODIVERSITY HOT SPOTS

Click on the link below to view a map of the world depicting regions of biodiversity loss and to learn about areas where conservation initiatives are needed: http://www.biodiversitya-z.org/content/biodiversity-hotspots (UNEP-WCMC 2014)

Some people argue the planet and all its life forms are an open market for human consumption and use. Without consideration for the use and transformation of the physical environment, people are altering and diminishing natural resources. The changes people make to nature cannot always be mitigated or restored. Additionally, alterations in the physical world result in changes in ecological and biological systems, including those of humans.

The loss of biodiversity directly and indirectly affects humans. The direct loss results in changes to and availability of food, raw materials, and medicines (Perry and Primrose 2015). This loss is directly correlated to the carbon cycle shifting pollination and biological controls effecting growth. Indirectly, the loss of biodiversity is changing climate, air quality, water availability, soil fertility, and the production of new agricultural products and medicines (Perry and Primrose 2015).

The social issue of biodiversity loss is linked to social structures and institutions that favor the vested interests of the powerful, underlying the practices of natural resource management and land use. In protecting their interests, the powerful impose their will upon biodiversity and promote consumption by the masses to make a profit

Sociological Application 4.2

Genetically Modified Food

Watch the short film entitled *Seeds of Freedom*: http://www.seedsoffreedom.info/

Research the following websites: http://www.etcgroup.org/issues/seeds-genetic-diversity http://www.navdanya.org/

Write a two-page reaction paper explaining your responses to the following questions:

1. Summarize the information you viewed and read.

2. Explain your reaction to the topic and why you think about the topic this way.

3. Judge, analyze, and evaluate the issues about the topic using citations and references.

4. Identify and discuss polarizing issues about the topic.

5. Include your opinions on the topic with evidence to support and justify your thinking.

and increase wealth (Perry and Primrose 2015). Social changes and government regulations to mitigate and restore biodiversity most impact and constrain the powerful in order to alter current social practices and conserve biodiversity.

Technology Gap

In the post-industrial or information age we are currently in, virtual space is just as important if not more so than physical space. Accessing this space can prove to be very challenging to many populations, particularly those in poorer communities. As the virtual world has developed and become an integral part of the way societies function, a technology gap or digital divide has emerged. The **digital divide** "is a social issue referring to the differing amount of information between those who have access to the Internet (especially broadband access) and those who do not have access" (Internet World Stats 2016). Multiple concerns exist regarding Internet access, including cost and quality of access. Being on the wrong side of the digital divide can look many different ways, such as having to work with a low performing computer, using dialup or narrowband connections, having limited access to technical assistance, and having reduced access to subscription-based services.

Because the Internet and other information and communications technologies (ICT) have reshaped how people function on a daily basis, some arguments have been made that these technologies and access to them is just as critical as access to a telephone or being able to read.

©smonkey/Shutterstock.com

Governments around the world invested in heavily in literacy and phone lines to ensure that their citizens have the benefits of both. Still just are there are disparities in the quality of phone lines and literacy rates from country to another, the same is true for ICTs. Considerable differences persist in average and maximum connection speeds, Internet penetration and broadband adaptation and mobile usage across country and not surprisingly, it is low-income countries that are typically on the wrong side of the divide. Within countries the divide is more pronounced in poor inner city areas and rural communities. Of course, not all aspects of the divide are connected to economic issues. Populations with certain disabilities must also have resources invested in providing them with more consistent and high quality access to the Internet and other ICTs (IWS 2016).

Bridging the technology gap or digital divide is considered an important goal around the world, as it has become necessary to have access to the Internet to ensure economic equality as more and more businesses and services operate a larger share of their activities online. Access to the Internet has also become essential for social mobility purposes, since using the Internet is required in most school settings, even at the primary level in many cases, but certainly at the secondary level and beyond. Using the Internet is also an essential tool when launching a search for employment. New economies are emerging through the use of the Internet, but populations who are struggling to access the Internet at a basic level are being left further and further behind. Recent research indicates that most people are unaware of the new economies that are emerging online, but awareness of such activities varies across demographic groups with higher-educated and higher-income populations being more aware of these new economies and the language used to discuss them (Smith 2016). Efforts to bridge this gap vary from one country to another, but there are some programs with a global mission such as One Laptop per Child and Close the Gap, which have a goal to provide access to computers to children in developing and emerging countries around the world.

Evaluating Critical Thinking and Credibility

In this module, we examined the influence of money and politics on human social life. At times, we find our economic pursuits and political affiliations impact the quality of life of others. In our pursuit of happiness and our drive to obtain the American Dream, we often ignore the influence that ego and self-interest have on the world around us. When people focus on individual pursuits and greed, the result has significant consequences for all life on the planet.

1. Think back on the social issues addressed in this module.
2. Discuss how self-deception and self-justification keep society from solving the issues presented.
3. Explain the pitfalls of egocentrism and how the personal interests of a powerful few affect the lives of the masses.
4. Describe methods for combating prejudice and discrimination when economic and political gains are at play.

Theoretical Analysis

As we use theoretical paradigms to examine the social world, we must be mindful of how each theory focuses on a particular level of analysis. Combined, the six paradigms offer a comprehensive understanding of the social structure. Individually, each paradigm provides insight into the influence of the social world on thinking and behavior and vice versa. The theories enhance critical thought by making us analyze and evaluate the social world from different levels of analysis to develop a comprehensive understanding of the human condition and the social issues we face.

Using a macrosociological perspective, **functionalists** examine the social world. This paradigm focuses on understanding the purpose or function of our social structure including the influence of our social systems, institutions, organizations, and processes on society. In examining politics and the economy, a functionalist will study the relevance of the social world, including systems of power and governance, why they were created, how they are operating, and if they are meeting expectations.

Conflict theorists also employ a macrosociological perspective to observe the social world. Conflict theory investigates competing groups and their struggle over resources. Using the conflict paradigm to analyze politics and the economy will focus on the divergence between the rich (i.e., power elite) and the poor and the power of money and influence.

In continuing examination of the social structure, **feminists** use a macrosociological approach to observe the social world. Feminists explore the lives and experiences of women and minority groups, including levels of oppression and discrimination they encounter. Application of the feminist paradigm to politics and the economy focuses on the history and inequity of women and minorities in these systems, including levels of governance and decision-making.

Environmental theorists provide a macrosociological perspective on the evolution of society. This paradigm considers how social groups evolve and adapt over time, in response to changes in the physical and social context. In studying politics and the economy, these theorists research the influence of social change, including the creation and development of policies, laws, and social movements in response to the political and economic environment.

Using a microsociological perspective **symbolic interactionists** evaluate the thinking and behavior of individuals. This paradigm focuses on identifying the labels, stereotypes, and symbolism associated within the social structure. When making observations around political ideology and economic theory, interactionists will explore the interpretation and meaning understood by individuals and groups involved and impacted by these systems.

©JensHN/Shutterstock.com

Exchange theorists also apply a microsociological perspective to observe thinking and behavior of individuals in society. Exchange theorists investigate how people are interest driven and identify their motivation in thinking and behavior. In examining political ideology and economic theory, these theorists look at the influences, reasons, and rationale people use in political and economic decision-making.

Choose one of the following social problems presented in this module and explain the issue and its impact on society:

- Campaign Finance
- Corporate Welfare
- War Profiteers
- Media Control
- Climate Change
- Biodiversity
- Environmental Racism
- Technology Gap

Analyze the problem using the six theoretical paradigms. Provide specific examples from this module to justify your analysis.

- Functionalism
- Conflict theory
- Interactionism
- Feminism
- Exchange theory
- Environmental theory

Social Policy

Social policy involves studying sociology, politics, and economics to understand how governments and society address social issues around well-being and justice. By studying social policy, we are able to recognize the causes of social problems and the solutions people attempt to implement in response. In the field of sociology, we examine social policy with the aim of improving or reforming society. A misconception among people is that solving social issues, including those controlled by money and power, requires financial resources to create change. A quote attributed to Anthropologist Margaret Mead serves as a reminder: "Never doubt that a small group of thoughtful, committed, citizens can change the world. Indeed, it is the only thing that ever has" (Sommers and Dineen 1984:158). In a practical way, Nipun Mehta, founder of *ServiceSpace*, a volunteer organization that supports generosity-driven projects, explains how people are participating in service opportunities throughout the world to create social change: https://youtu.be/BoV23TJe4UM

1. What lessons can you learn from the stories of generosity and service presented by Nipum Mehta?
2. How is it possible for people to create social change without money?
3. How might microsociological acts (interactions between people) lead to macrosociological changes (systems, organizations, and processes) in society?
4. What impact does intrinsic or internal motivation have on social change and the gift economy?

To learn more, visit *ServiceSpace* at http://www.servicespace.org

Social Movements and Reform

Social movements require group action and seek to address political or social issues. Social movements develop over time and eventually bureaucratize into a formal organization (Tilly 1977).

Once a movement achieves success or is no longer supported, the organization adapts or evolves its goal and vision to garner new support or simply declines and eventually ceases to exist.

Throughout history, numerous social movements throughout the world have combatted political and economic unrest. Today, many movements use the Internet to create awareness and cultivate membership for their causes. The Revolution in Cairo led by the April 6th Youth Movement in 2008 used Facebook and YouTube to organize a national protest. See their story on PBS Frontline at: http://www.pbs.org/wgbh/pages/frontline/revolution-in-cairo/.

1. Think about the political and economic injustices we discussed in this module.

2. How would you create public awareness about one of these issues to develop a social movement?

3. If you had to create a short, precise statement or sound bite about the issue in 140 characters or less, how would you frame the message of your movement? What would you trend?

4. Develop a list of methods in addition to social media and the Internet, you would use to help gather people to discuss the issue face-to-face and develop solutions for addressing it?

5. How would you keep people informed and committed to working on the issue for a long period of time, maybe even years?

References

Barlett, Donald L. and James B. Steele. 1998. "Corporate Welfare." *Time, Inc.*, November 9, pp. 36–54. Retrieved June 25, 2016 (http://www.cnn.com/ALLPOLITICS/time/1998/11/02/corp.welfare.html).

Brockovich, Erin. 2015. "Erin Brockovich: Consumer Advocate." Retrieved June 27, 2016 (http://www.brockovich.com/).

Carabelli, Anna Maria and Mario Aldo Cedrini. 2013. "Further Issues on the Keynes-Hume Connection Relating to the Theory of Financial Markets in the General Theory." *European Journal of the History of Economic Thought* 20(6):1071–1100.

Chomsky, Noam. 2002. *Media Control: The Spectacular Achievements of Propaganda*. 2nd edition. New York: Seven Stories Press.

Clark, Lara P., Dylan B. Millet, and Julian D. Marshall. 2014. "National Patterns in Environmental Injustice and Inequality: Outdoor NO_2 Air Pollution in the United States." *PLOS/One*. Retrieved June 21, 2016 (http://journals.plos.org/plosone/article?id=10.1371/journal.pone.0094431).

Department of Justice. 2014. "Defense Contractor Agrees to Pay $27.5 Million to Settle Overbilling Allegations." *Justice News*, December 19.

Department of Justice. 2016. "Lockheed Martin Agrees to Pay $5 Million to Settle Alleged Violations of the False Claims Act and the Resource Conservation and Recovery Act." *Justice News*, February 29.

Deryugina, Tatyana and Olga Shurchkov. 2016. "The Effect of Information Provision on Public Consensus about Climate Change." *PLoS One* 11(4):1–14.

Federal Election Commission (FEC). 2016a. "Bipartisan Campaign Reform Act of 2002." Retrieved June 24, 2016. (http://www.fec.gov/pages/bcra/bcra_update.shtml).

Federal Election Commission (FEC). 2016b. "2016 Presidential Campaign Finance." Retrieved June 24, 2016. (http://fec.gov/disclosurep/pnational.do)

Free Press. 2016. "Fighting Media Consolidation." Retrieved June 23, 2016 (http://www.freepress.net/media-consolidation).

"Government Spends More on Corporate Welfare Subsidies than Social Welfare Programs." 2013. Think by Numbers. Retrieved June 25, 2016 (http://thinkbynumbers.org/government-spending/corporate-welfare/corporate-vs-social-welfare/).

Greenwald, Robert and Derrick Crowe. 2012. "You Can Be a Patriot Or a Profiteer...But You Can't Be Both." *Huffpost Politics*, April 27.

Internet World Stats: Usage and Population Statistics (IWS). 2016. "The Digital Divide, ICT, and Broadband Internet." Retrieved June 23, 2016. (http://www.Internetworldstats.com/links10.htm).

John Birch Society. 2015. "Big Business Gets Big Subsidies from Washington." *New American*, April 6, p. 8.

Kreitler, Jason, Carrie Schloss, Oliver Soong, Lee Hannah, and Frank Davis. 2015. "Conservation Planning for Offsetting the Impacts of Development: A Case Study of Biodiversity and Renewable Energy in the Mojave Desert." *PLoS One* 10(10):1–15.

Konradi, Amanda and Martha Schmidt. 2004. *Reading between the Lines*. New York: McGraw-Hill.

Lake Research Partners and Chesapeake Beach Consulting. 2014. "Research Findings on the People's Pledge. Retrieved June 30, 2016 (https://www.scribd.com/doc/236631862/Recent-research-findings-on-the-People-s-Pledge).

Marx, Karl. 1859. *A Contribution to the Critique of Political Economy*. Moscow: Progress Publishers.

McMahon, Tamsin. 2014. "Toying with Corporate Welfare." *Maclean's*, February 10, pp. 46–49.

MEA (Millennium Ecosystem Assessment). 2005. "Ecosystems and Human Well-being: Biodiversity Synthesis." *World Resources Institute*, pp. 1–16.

Miranda, Marie Lynn, Sharon E. Edwards, Martha H. Keating, and Christopher J. Paul. 2011. "Making the Environmental Justice Grade: The Relative Burden of Air Pollution Exposure in the United States." *International Journal of Environmental Research and Public Health 8: 1755–1771.*

Montanaro, Domenico, Rachel Wellford, and Simone Pathe. 2014. "Money is a Pretty Good Predictor of Who Will Win Elections." PBS NewsHour: Politics: The Morning Line. Retrieved June 24, 2016 (http://www.pbs.org/newshour/updates/money-pretty-good-predictor-will-win-elections/).

Murray, Bobbi. 2003. "Money for Nothing." *The Nation*, September 1–8, pp. 25–28.

OpenSecrets.org. 2016. "What is a PAC?" Center for Responsive Politics. Retrieved June 23, 2016 (https://www.opensecrets.org/pacs/pacfaq.php).

Orum, Paul, Richard Moore, Michele Roberts, and Joaquin Sanchez. 2014. "Who's In Danger? Race, Poverty, and Chemical Disasters: A Demographic Analysis of Chemical Disaster Vulnerability Zones." Environmental Justice and Health Alliance for Chemical Policy Reform. Retrieved June 22, 2016 (http://comingcleaninc.org/assets/media/images/Reports/Who%27s%20in%20Danger%20Report%20FINAL.pdf).

Orwell, George. 1946. *Animal Farm*. New York: Harcourt Brace Jovanovich.

Perry, Neil and David Primrose. 2015. "Heterodox Economics and the Diversity Crisis." *Journal of Australian Political Economy* 75:133–152.

Principles of Environmental Justice. 1991. Environmental Justice/Environmental Racism. Retrieved June 24, 2016 (http://www.ejnet.org/ej/principles.html).

Robbins, Richard. 2007. *Global Problems and the Culture of Capitalism.* Upper Saddle River, NJ: Prentice Hall.

Roush, Wade. 2010. "The Story of SIRI, from Birth at SRI to Acquisition by Apple—Virtual Personal Assistants Go Mobile." *Xconomy*, June 14, 2010.

Shaftel, Holly. 2016. "NASA Global Climate Change: Vital Signs of the Planet." Retrieved June 16, 2016 (http://climate.nasa.gov/effects/).

Sommers, Frank G. and Tana Dineen. 1984. *Curing Nuclear Madness.* London: Methuen Publishing Ltd.

Smith, Aaron. 2016. "Shared, Collaborative, and On Demand: The Digital Economy." Pew Research Center: Internet, Science, and Tech. Retrieved June 24, 2016 (http://www.pewInternet.org/2016/05/19/the-new-digital-economy/).

Tilly, Charles. 1977. *From Mobilization to Revolution.* Ann Arbor, MI: Center for Research on Social Organization, University of Michigan.

Transforming World Atlas. 2016. Bank of America Merrill Lynch. Retrieved June 25, 2016 (http://www.bofaml.com/content/dam/boamlimages/documents/articles/ID16-305/bofaml_transforming_world_atlas_2nd_edition.pdf).

UNEP-WCMC. 2014. "Biodiversity A-Z." Retrieved December 28, 2015 (http://www.biodiversitya-z.org).

War Profiteering Prevention Act of 2007. 2007. H.R. 400, 110th Congress.

Weber, Max. [1921] 2013. *Economy and Society,* edited by Guenther Roth and Claus Wittich. Berkeley, CA: University of California Press.

Weigley, Samuel. 2013. "10 companies Profiting the Most from War." *USA Today*, March 10, 2013.

Do you know the terms?

Using the list provided below, create a personal dictionary of key terms and concepts presented in this module. Include the term, phonetic spelling (if needed), and definition in your own words. Next, provide a real world example of the term or concept based on your previous knowledge or new information you learned in this module to help re-enforce learning.

Biodiversity	Genetically modified food
Campaign finance	Hegemony
Climate change	Media control
Conflict theory	Move to Amend
Corporate welfare	Political action committee
Digital divide	Political economy of place
Economic theory	Political parties
Economy	Power
Environmental theory	Symbolic interactionism
Exchange theory	War profiteers
Feminism	World systems theory
Functionalism	

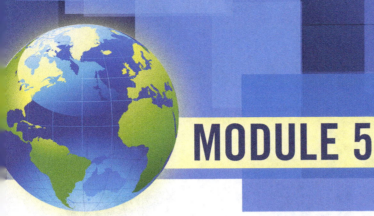

MODULE 5

Crime and Violence

Deviance and Social Control

As we learned in Module 3, **norms** are standards for behavior in a given society. Adherence to these norms is critical to the operation of any society. Social control mechanisms are techniques and strategies established by society to prevent members of the society from violating norms or breaking rules. **Sanctions** reinforce the social control mechanisms. Negative sanctions or **penalties** are issued when norms are violated, while positive sanctions or **rewards** are issued when norms are upheld or societal expectations are met. The goal of any social control mechanism is to encourage conformity with peers and obedience to authority figures and to discourage deviant or norm-violating behavior. Thus, **deviance** (i.e., rule breaking) and **social control** are the two sides of a coin.

There is a tendency to focus on the rule breaking aspect of deviance, but there are multiple perspectives or views regarding deviant behavior. The most common form of deviance is **statistical**. Any variation from the average or norm constitutes deviance. From this perspective, people who are shorter or taller than the average height in a given society are viewed as deviant, although no rules have been broken or violated. Another way to think about deviance is from the **absolute or moralistic** perspective. From this perspective, deviance is about right versus wrong and knowing the difference. The **medical/social-pathological** perspective of deviance assumes that due to

©iQoncept/Shutterstock.com

some medical impairment an individual is not able to understand what is considered acceptable or "right" and what is considered unacceptable or "wrong." Finally, deviance is relative. What constitutes deviant behavior varies by time, place, situation, and social status. This **relativistic** perspective of deviance captures the essence of the social foundations of deviance.

The **foundation of social deviance** has three components and two of these are essential elements of the relativistic perspective. First, deviance varies according to social norms. As the relativistic perspective suggests, what is considered deviant varies depending upon what social norms are in place and this may vary from society to society (place), from one era to another even

TABLE 10

3 Components of Social Deviance
1. Deviance varies according to social norms.
2. A deviant identity is established once others define a person as deviant.
3. Norms and how rule breaking is defined involve social power.

within the same society (time), from one situation to another (situation), and from one person to another (social status). Second, a deviant identity is established once others define a person as deviant. It is not what a person does that makes him or her deviant; it is how others respond to what he or she has done. If no one witnesses the behavior, it cannot be identified as deviant. Furthermore, if the behavior is witnessed, but it is not labeled as deviant, then the person who committed the act is not considered deviant. Finally, how norms are established and how rule breaking is defined is determined by those who possess social power. Those with enough power to establish the norms are also able to determine when the norms or rules have been broken or violated and who is labeled as deviant. As the relativistic perspective suggests, individuals with power are able to use their resources to avoid being labeled as deviant when they break the rules, while others with less social status or power who commit the same actions would be labeled as deviant.

Social Issues

State Violence

Government and its subsidiaries maintain the legal authority to commit violent acts against people for repression and control. **State violence** or authorized acts of violence against people by government or its institutions are often legitimized by claiming they are necessary to maintain security and order. Institutions and organizations authorized to use violence or force generally include the military, police, courts, schools, and social welfare agencies, including child protective services.

©CRM/Shutterstock.com

A state or government maintains the power to use violence against enemies, other states (e.g., war), and its citizens. In Latin America, state violence is deployed against children as part of its anti-gang policies to curtail youth violence. In 2006, the *World Report on Violence against Children* (http://www.unviolencestudy.org/) found state violence and corruption in Latin America are directly associated with violence in communities in the context of "law and public order," including the mistreatment, abuse, and neglect of children in the care of the state.

Declaration of War and Authorized Use of Military Force

A **declaration of war** and authorized use of military force is formalized when a national government authorizes violent conflict between opposing or threatening groups and states. On a national level, the power to steer or direct acts of war is decided by the government and influenced by its institutions (e.g., military) and other powerful groups (e.g., corporations). C. Wright Mills (1956) defined these influential political, military, and economic leaders as the **power elite**. G. William Domhoff (1998) proposed the corporate community (e.g., executives of the largest corporations, banks, investment firms, and agribusiness) work together to determine and position political leaders and public officials using their "structural economic power" to influence policy, including declarations of war.

In the United States, Congress and the President have formerly enacted war 11 times, authorizing the killing of enemy combatants, seizure of enemy property, and apprehension of enemy aliens (Congressional Research Service 2014). President Dwight D. Eisenhower recognized the danger of the armed forces and defense industries or the **military-industrial complex** to influence and direct war and the authorized use of military force for economic gain. As a general in WWII, President Eisenhower was aware how industries benefitted from the sale of weapons and other supplies and services during wartime. In his farewell address, President Eisenhower recognized how military leaders and the weapons industry hold the power to influence and set a course for war, resulting in increased violence and authorized use of military force for profit (see President Eisenhower's Farewell Address at: https://youtu.be/OyBNmecVtdU).

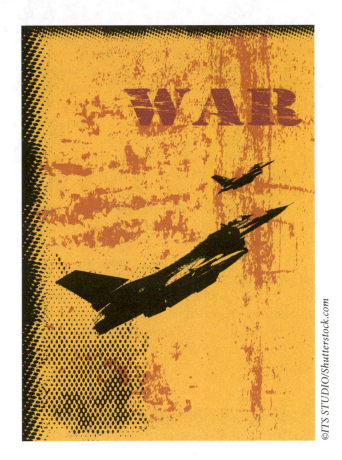

©ITS STUDIO/Shutterstock.com

Terrorism

The use and threatened use of violence for political, religious, or ideological means is considered **terrorism**, and it is not a new or recent phenomenon, as terrorism has existed since the beginning of the human race. The purpose of terrorism, as a tactic, is to inflate fear and submission through violence or the threat of violence and may refer to both a mode of governing as well as opposing governments (Herman 1986). Terrorist entities may manifest internally (domestic or from within a state or nation) or externally (international or from a nation state or government) and work in isolation or through networks. Terrorist groups justify the use of violence to promote their beliefs or create political change. Terrorism symbolizes power, making terrorists feel powerful, important, and righteous. This sense of power and climate of fear fuels a group's strength and solidarity.

After the September 11, 2001 terrorist attacks in the United States, President George W. Bush declared a *War on Terror* (see the president's address at: http://abcnews.go.com/Archives/video/sept-20-2001-bush-declares-war-terror-10995502). This was the first time in U.S. history when war was declared on a tactic. Previous declarations of war were against specific groups, countries, or regions of people, but the *War on Terror* focused on fighting terrorism, which legitimized and authorized a never-ending war, institutionalizing the military-industrial complex.

Additionally, the terrorist attacks on 9/11 imprinted prejudice and discrimination against Middle Eastern and Muslim people. People from Middle Eastern countries and followers of Islam are now viewed and questioned as terrorists throughout the world and in the United States, despite the fact that terrorism is committed by a variety of individuals from various social class,

---

Sociological Application 5.2

Labeling Terrorists

From September 11, 2001 through the end of May 2016, more domestic terrorist acts have been committed by far right wing Americans than jihadists.

1. Check out the terrorist attack incidents in the United States since 9/11 at: http://securitydata.newamerica.net/extremists/deadly-attacks.html

2. Visit the FBI Terrorism website: https://www.fbi.gov/about-us/investigate/terrorism

3. Given the number of terrorist acts committed by far right wing Americans, why do people continue to stereotype Middle Eastern and Muslim people as "terrorists" in the United States? Why isn't the same stereotype applied to all Americans on the right of the political spectrum?

4. Why are Middle Eastern and Muslim people continuously considered jihadists (Islamic militants) in America? How are these stereotypes reinforced? What examples can you find supporting these stereotypes? What examples do you know of that contrast with these stereotypes?

5. What is the value and importance of labeling Middle Eastern and Muslim people as terrorists? Why do people avoid asking the religious affiliation and beliefs of far right wing terrorists? How do Caucasian men benefit from far right wing terrorists being labeled "lone wolves"?

6. Read these two brief articles about the June 2016 incident in Orlando: http://www.juancole.com/2016/06/rightwing-homophobia-terrorism.html and http://www.nytimes.com/interactive/2016/06/13/us/politics/politicians-respond-to-orlando-nightclub-attack.html?_r=0.

7. How would you classify this particular incident? Do you consider the individual responsible, Omar Mateen, a jihadist or right-wing extremist? Why?

religious, ethnic, and political backgrounds. For example, since 9/11, right-wing terrorists have killed 48 people in the United States; however, the spotlight and labels associated with these murderers are defined within the context of "lone wolf" and "terrorist" stereotypes about the offenders—young, predominantly Caucasian men who are not conceived by the public or the media as part of a collective to be feared and profiled (New America 2016).

Genocide

One of the most horrendous acts against human rights is the deliberate killing of a large group of people with the intent to eliminate their ethnic, racial, religious, or national existence. One of the first genocides recorded in the 20th century occurred in Asia Minor from 1915–1923, in which the Ottoman Turkish Government targeted Armenians, Assyrians, and Greeks living in the Ottoman Empire for extermination. However, the term "genocide" was not used until 1944 when attorney Raphael Lemkin (combining *geno-*, from the Greek word for race or tribe, with *-cide*, derived from the Latin word for killing) coined the word genocide and "cited the 1915 annihilation of Armenians as a seminal example of genocide" (Auron 2004:9). The term was also used to describe the Nazi systematic mass murder of European Jews from 1933–1945 (United States

©*Everett Historical/Shutterstock.com*

Holocaust Memorial Museum 2016). In 1948, the United Nations convened and defined the international law on genocide (http://www.oas.org/dil/1948_Convention_on_the_Prevention_and_Punishment_of_the_Crime_of_Genocide.pdf):

Acts of genocide have been committed throughout the world including the mass murder of Native Americans in the United States. The most predominant mass killings were of Armenians (during WWI), Jews (during WWII), Cambodians (during the Vietnam War), Tutsis (in Rwanda), and Darfuris (Sudan) (see summary of past genocides at: http://endgenocide.org/learn/past-genocides/). Though millions of people have been killed through genocide, many political leaders and nationalists deny their "crimes against humanity" as defined by international law.

Excerpt from the *1948 UN Convention on the Prevention and Punishment of Genocide*

Article I: The Contracting Parties confirm that genocide, whether committed in time of peace or in time of war, is a crime under international law which they undertake to prevent and to punish.

Article II: In the present Convention, genocide means any of the following acts committed with intent to destroy, in whole or in part, a national, ethnical, racial or religious group, as such:

(a) Killing members of the group;

(b) Causing serious bodily or mental harm to members of the group;

(c) Deliberately inflicting on the group conditions of life calculated to bring about its physical destruction in whole or in part;

(d) Imposing measures intended to prevent births within the group;

(e) Forcibly transferring children of the group to another group.

Predatory Violence

Violence is quite prevalent in U.S. culture. Rates of lethal violence are higher in the United States compared to other Western, industrialized nations (Winslow and Zhang 2008). The nature of the violence dictates how society responds to it. Killing and murder are not synonymous. Killing is not murder when it is considered moral and just or defined as lawful for the protection and security of society (Curra 2014).

Predatory violence is premeditated violence of an instrumental nature. It is violence that has been carefully plotted to achieve specific goals (Declercq and Audanaert 2011; Meloy 2006). It is treated differently than affective violence, which is impulsive, reactive, and emotionally charged (Declercq and Audanaert 2011; Hanlon, Brook, Stratton, Jensen, and Rubin 2013). An act of predatory violence is not easily excused as **medicalized deviance**, because the perpetrator was cognitively capable of planning and executing the violent act.

The Bureau of Justice Statistics (BJS) publishes the nature, trends, and patterns of murder and non-negligent manslaughter. The United States collects data from the Federal Bureau of Investigation's Supplementary Homicide Reports (SHR) and Centers for Disease Control and Prevention's National Vital Statistics System Fatal Injury Reports (NVSS) to track information on homicides. The NVSS shows a higher rate and number

TABLE 11

Comparing the NVSS Fatal Injury Reports and the UCR Supplementary Homicide Reports

	NVSS	SHR
Purpose	Track all deaths	Track crime statistics
Reporting Source	State vital registrars	Law enforcement agencies
Initial Report	Death certificate	Police report
Reporting Responsibility	Medical examiners and coroners	Law enforcement officers
Homicide Definition	Injuries inflicted by another person with intent to injure or kill by any means.	Willful killing of one human being by another, includes murders & non-negligent manslaughters
Reporting is	Mandatory	Voluntary
Data Collection Methods	Manner/cause of death determined by medical examiners/coroners; demographic information is recorded by funeral directors on death certificates	In most states, reports from individual law enforcement agencies are compiled monthly by state-level agencies and then forwarded to the FBI

BJS 2014

TABLE 12

Homicide Rates in the NVSS and SHR, 1981–2011

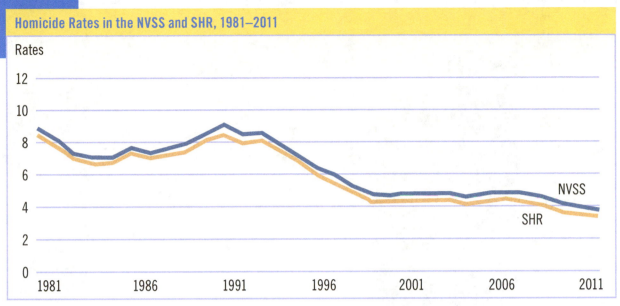

Note: SHR data include intentional homicides known to law enforcement and exclude justifiable homicides and nonnegligent manslaughter. NVSS data include all homicides committed by civilians (regardless of intent) and exclude homicides due to legal intervention. Both data sources exclude homicides resulting from operations of war and the terrorist attacks of September 11, 2001. Rates are calculated as the number of homicides per 100,000 U.S. residents. SHR rates are weighted to the annual number of homicide victims reported in the FBI's Uniform Crime Reports.

BJS 2014

of murders compared to the SHR as a result in data collection variance in coverage, scope, and voluntary nature of the design (BJS 2014). Despite these differences, both data sources show a decline in national homicides.

Mass Shootings

Mass shootings have become all too common in the United States in recent years. To be deemed a mass shooting, at least four or more individuals, not including the shooter, must be shot and/or killed in a single event in the same location and at the same general time (Gun Violence Archive 2016). Almost a third of all mass shootings around the world between 1966 and 2012 occurred in the United States (Lankford 2016), although the United States constitutes only 5% of the world's population. The average number of mass shootings each year has been steadily increasing. The deadliest mass shooting in U.S. history occurred in June of 2016. Forty-nine people were killed and another 50 were injured at a gay nightclub

in Orlando, Florida, where patrons were enjoying "Latin Night" and celebrating Pride Month (Willingham 2016).

As these shootings have continued to occur with regularity, a pattern has emerged. The nation grieves, displays shock and outrage, and then subsequent discussions about how to prevent such events from occurring turn into heated political debates about gun control. Thus far, no significant legislation to change gun control

FIGURE 16   2010 EXPENDITURES BY GUN-ISSUE NONPROFITS

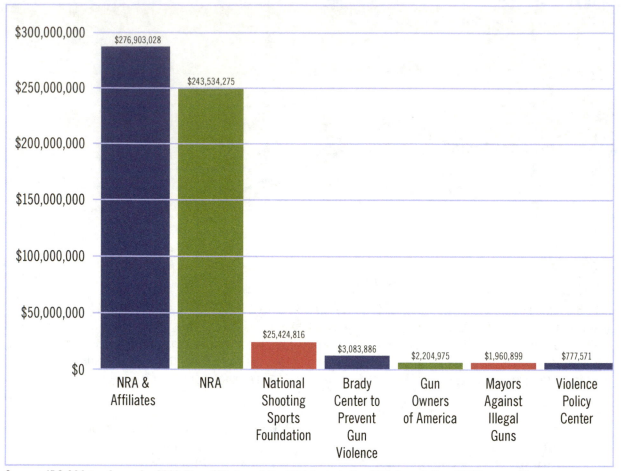

Source: *IRS 990 tax forms for 2010*. The affiliates of the NRA include the NRA Foundation [2010 expenditures: $26,539,658], NRA Freedom Action Center [$2,541,434], NRA Civil Rights Defense Fund [$749,265] and NRA Special Contribution Fund [$3,538,396].)

laws has passed since 1994 (Gettings and McNiff 2000–2016), despite the fact that most Americans, including most gun owners, say they want stricter gun control laws. If the public wants stricter gun control laws, why hasn't Congress passed any gun control legislation in over two decades? Many political pundits suggest that the National Rifle Association (NRA) has used its economic power to lobby Congress members and convince them that it is in their best interests to cast gun friendly votes. Ironically, though after each mass shooting, gun sales increase as discussions about gun control increase (Willingham 2016).

GUN CONTROL DEMANDS

An unprecedented sit-in led by House Democrats occurred on the floor of the House of Representatives on June 22, 2016 to bring attention to the issue of unregulated gun access and force a Congressional vote on four gun control bills being blocked by House Republican. Watch online: https://youtu.be/Ykll-2ieYCk

Infanticide

Infanticide is the murder or killing of a child between the age of one week old and one year old. Although it sounds reprehensible, every culture or society has practiced some form of infanticide for various reasons (Moran 2003). In the United States, there is a tendency to associate this practice with less developed countries, but the reality is that infanticide is a common occurrence in the modern United States as well.

The reasons for committing infanticide vary from society to society, but traditional explanations include human sacrifice, population control, poverty, devaluation of females, birth defects, illegitimacy, and superstition. The methods of committing infanticide have changed over time, which reflects shifts in cultural beliefs. Abandonment/exposure is the oldest method of committing infanticide, while suffocation is the most common method. Other methods include drowning, neglect, and abuse. Currently, the most common methods of infanticide are head trauma, such as that which results from shaken baby syndrome, drowning, suffocation, and strangulation (Moran 2003).

High rates of female infanticide in China and India have created large sex-ratio imbalances. The loss of millions of female children has made it difficult for many males in those countries to find partners to marry. Currently, in the United States, the typical parent who kills a child is poor, single, less than 19 years old, a rural resident, and lacks a high school diploma. Other risk factors, especially for mothers, include a history of repeated drug and alcohol use, a history of depression, a childhood history of parental neglect and abuse, being involved with an abusive partner, not receiving prenatal care, a history of self-abuse, and limited social support. Efforts to reduce infanticide center around providing more social support for parents and treating mental health disorders before they contribute to tragic outcomes such as infanticide (Moran 2003).

Executions

The death penalty continues to be controversial in the United States, as serious concerns about whether it is applied equitably have been raised since at least the 1960s. Thirty-one states mete out death sentences. Over the last 40 years, almost 1,500 prisoners have been executed. The demographic data indicates that African Americans are over-represented in terms of those executed. African Americans constitute about 13% of the U.S. population, but they account for over a third (34.5%) of all convicted criminals executed during this time period. African Americans comprise 43% of inmates who are on death row and executions are much more prevalent in the South, where African Americans reside in greater numbers. The death penalty is much more likely to be meted out when the victim is white. Whites are the murder victims in about 50% of the cases; however, for cases that resulted in an execution, 76% of the murder victims were white (DPIC 2016).

The frequency of death sentences has been declining year after year. Perhaps this reflects the efforts of those who seek to curtail this form of punishment due to its uneven application across racial groups. The decline in death sentences may also

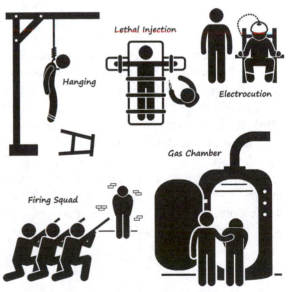

©Leremy/Shutterstock.com

reflect that there is growing evidence that the death penalty is not deterring criminal behavior (DPIC 2016). Many states are beginning to question the use of the death penalty, because it is extremely expensive. There are also concerns about wrongful executions, especially considering that the number of inmates exonerated and released from death row has increased from an average of three per year from 1973–1999, to an average of five per year from 2000–2011 (DPIC 2016). Recently, there have been concerns about the safety of the drugs used to perform lethal injections in some states (Zimmer et al. 2007). Altogether, these issues have made the U.S. public hesitant to support the death penalty, with 61% of the population supporting alternatives to the death penalty (DPIC 2016).

Modern Slavery

Over 30 million people are enslaved around the world today (Fisher 2013). Many of these "slaves" are bonded by debt and have pledged themselves or a member of their family into slavery as repayment for some debt owed. Debts are passed down through generations because payments of debt are rarely fulfilled (Bales 2002). Others of these "slaves" are victims of organized crime and are smuggled across countries to be sold.

ENSLAVED POPULATIONS

Click on the link below to view a map of the world depicting regions, including the United States, where people are enslaved and to learn about who is impacted by the practice of modern slavery: https://www.washingtonpost.com/news/worldviews/wp/2013/10/17/this-map-shows-where-the-worlds-30-million-slaves-live-there-are-60000-in-the-u-s/

(Fisher 2013)

Though every country in the world has made it illegal to own and exercise control over someone, laws are not enforced. Slavery has become a form of organized crime with centralized enterprises

run by criminals. Slaveholders and slaves seek economic opportunities; however, people who become slaves seldom know that they will lose their free will and suffer psychological degradation (Bales 2002).

Slaves develop relationships with slaveholders or masters. Out of desperation, some slaves seek refuge in the control of a "master." On occasion, the life of a slave appears far better than a life of poverty. Slaveholders psychologically manipulate slaves and reinforce mutual dependence (Bales 2002). Slaves are told they will be provided food, clothing, shelter, and safety under a master's care.

In many underdeveloped and impoverished countries, women are socialized to accept cultural norms of control and compliance making a life into slavery acceptable. Slaveholders simply think of themselves as businessmen helping those in need by providing security and resources (Bales 2002). This ideology is viewed as necessary in areas of the world with economic instability and limited resources.

Slavery must be combated on several fronts. People fall into slavery out of desperation and survival. Underdeveloped areas of the world need resources and economic stability, including access to education and health care, so people have other opportunities for survival. For individuals who escape slavery, rehabilitation systems with appropriate supports are needed to help former slaves adjust to and sustain freedom (Bales 2002). Most importantly, governments must enforce anti-slavery laws and stop human trafficking.

Forced Labor

Of the many forms of modern slavery, **forced labor** refers to the engagement of work or services against personal will, coerced by fear, punishment, and/or retribution. Forced labor is involuntary servitude. The practice of trafficking forced labor in the United States was not criminalized until 2000 with the passage of the *Victims of Trafficking and Violence Protection Act* (Owens, Dank, Breaux, Banuelos, Farrell, Pfeffer, Bright, Heitsmith, and McDevitt 2015).

Though they are approximately 60,000 cases of forced labor in the United States annually, victims are rarely familiar with the individuals involved in their exploitation (Fisher 2013). Law enforcement agencies are the most viable sources of data about perpetrators and their criminal networks, though not all incidences of labor trafficking are investigated in detail and suspect information gathered (Owens et al. 2015). In most cases, the employer or direct supervisor is the primary suspect in trafficking forced labor.

TABLE 13	
Industries of Exploitation	
Private residences	Assisted living facilities
Agriculture	Factories
Hospitality	Construction
Restaurants	Other (carnival, fairs, etc.)
Strip clubs/Massage parlors	

Owens et al. 2015

Sex Trafficking

The United States *Victims of Trafficking and Violence Protection Reauthorization Act of 2013* made a symbolic distinction between "sex" and "non-sex" trafficking bringing light to the difference of forced labor and forced prostitution (Peters 2013). **Sex trafficking** and forced prostitution produces a unique form of vulnerability and harm to victims, as it violates the personal freedom of consent to time, place, and type of sexual activity.

Forced prostitution is coerced by a third party and is involuntary prostitution. With the passage of the Victims of Trafficking and Violence Protection Reauthorization Act in 2013, the United States recognized the physical, psychological, and social consequences of being a victim of forced sex deserved special consideration as a severely immoral objectionable offense. Changes to the law recognized the rights of victims, who are primarily girls and women, shifting the cultural perspective of how they are treated and their rights acknowledged and protected.

©ChameleonsEye/Shutterstock.com

DOMESTIC MINOR SEX TRAFFICKING

According to Kotrla (2010), American youth are the most vulnerable to sex trafficking in the United States. Click on the link below to view Carissa's story about being homeless and forced into prostitution in Fresno, California: http://on.aol.com/video/carissa-517354558

Sociological Application 5.4

What is the impact of modern slavery?

Write a three-page paper discussing the impact of modern slavery on society focusing on the social analysis of the problem and potential remedies for change.

1. Research the **economic** impact of slavery. How does the practice of servitude affect the global economy? What affect does modern slavery have on your local community?

2. Research the **political** impact of slavery. Which countries and political organizations spread the practice of servitude and which do not? What is the political gain and costs of supporting such practices?

3. Research the **legal** impact of slavery. What laws has the United Nations developed to combat modern slavery? Which countries support these initiatives and have created their own? Which countries enforce anti-slavery laws and are they successful in stopping the practice of servitude?

4. Research the **social** impact of slavery. What customs, traditions, and other social dynamics re-enforce slavery? How has the perspective of slavery changed over time? Where is the practice of servitude still viewed as acceptable and functional in society?

5. After completing your research, provide two **changes or solutions** to address modern slavery globally and in your community.

Organizational Deviance

Some deviant behavior occurs at a micro-level while other deviant behavior occurs at a macro-level. The tendency is to focus more upon deviance committed by individuals because it is easier to assign responsibility or blame to individuals who violate rules and/or laws. Deviance committed at the organizational level merits just as much attention, if not more, because it usually involves accessing the power structure of the organization to carry out the acts of deviance. The opportunity structure of an organization is a significant variable in the type of deviance that may occur (Curra 2014). For example, professional sports organizations are more susceptible to deviant behavior involving point shaving and securing rights to host or televise games.

THE FIFA SCANDAL

In 2015, officials and associates of *Fédération Internationale de Football Association* (FIFA) were indicted for corruption. Multiple executives of the world's governing body accepted bribes in exchange for hosting and television rights of The World Cup, the most-watched sporting event in the world. Check out the timeline of corruption at: https://youtu.be/Bw-bcnSivmM

Another interesting aspect of organizational deviance is that the deviant behavior under examination is carried out by the organization that is comprised of numerous individuals. Those individuals acting together may commit acts in the name of the organization that they would not commit as individuals. Additionally, organizational representatives may protect each other by concealing or covering up any deviance or crime that occurs (Curra 2014). The resources of the organization can be used to sustain the deviant behavior, which may increase and prolong the impact of the deviance.

Elite Deviance

There is a tendency to focus on street crime or index crimes because they involve harm to the person or property. Media focuses on these types of crimes because they are sensational. The mantra, "If it bleeds, it leads," dictates what new stories are reported, so index crimes (murder, manslaughter, robbery, assault, forcible rape, arson, larceny-theft, auto vehicle theft, and burglary) dominate the news cycle. But crimes committed by the powerful are more likely to affect the average person. Why? Think about it. Are you more likely to be a victim of an index crime or a white collar or corporate crime? You are not robbed, burglarized or assaulted on a daily basis, but you do pay higher premiums each day due to insurance fraud and company theft.

White collar crime consists of occupational crime, which is when individuals commit crimes at their place of employment in conjunction with their daily activities, and corporate crime, which is when corporations violate laws in an effort to maximize profits. Occupational criminals are seeking to increase their personal wealth, while corporate criminals conduct activities that

WHITE COLLAR CRIMES

money laundering   fraud   embezzlement

insider trading   bribery   Ponzi schemes

forgery   identity theft   cybercrime

benefit the corporation. Examples of occupational crime include theft of company materials, embezzlement, forgery, counterfeiting, and insurance fraud. Examples of corporate crime include price fixing, antitrust violations, and security fraud (Friedrichs 2002). Several high profile examples of white collar crime have been highlighted in the media in recent years such as the Bernie Madoff Ponzi scheme (Yang 2014) and securities fraud, tax evasion, and insider trading committed by executives at major corporations such as Enron, Adelphia, and AIG (Markon and Frank 2002; Spitzer 2009;). Despite these high profile examples that the media paid attention to and brought to the public's awareness, most white collar crimes go unreported and unexamined due to a lack of resources to tackle what are usually very complicated crimes.

The fact that white collar crimes and corporate crimes are more likely to be committed by elite deviants, powerful and higher income individuals, makes it more likely that these crimes will not be treated as harshly as crimes committed by the typical street criminal. These elite deviants are in the position to determine what is considered deviant. When they break rules, deviant behavior has not occurred, because recall the first social foundation of deviance—it is not what you do that makes you deviant, but how others respond to what you do that makes your behavior deviant. Elite deviance may also be less examined because many corporations prefer to keep a low profile about such violations to avoid a potential scandal.

Prison Industrial Complex

The United States has the highest rate of incarceration among all industrialized nations (www. sentencingproject.org). Over two million U.S. residents are currently incarcerated. This represents a 500% increase over the last several decades. Are U.S. citizens inherently more criminal than other populations around the world? If not, what accounts for such an inordinate increase in the number of incarcerated citizens? Many criminal justice experts argue this increase in the rate of incarceration was inevitable as the expenditures

on prisons have steadily increased (Doten 2010; Smith and Hattery 2010; Magnani 2011).

The number of prisons being built has risen steadily over the last several decades (Hattery and Smith 2008; Smith and Hattery 2006). The amount of dollars spent on building prisons and housing prisoners has increased during this same period. For example, in 1980, California's 10 prisons housed 25,000 prisoners at an annual cost of $604 million. By 2013, California had built 23 new prisons and housed more than 130,000 prisoners at an annual cost of approximately $10 billion (Knafo 2013). As the famous line from the film, *Field of Dreams* (1989), "If you build it, he (they) will come" suggests, growth will occur where resources are invested. When more and more resources are directed to the construction of prisons, investors like to see a return on their investment. The surest way to achieve the return on what is invested in prisons is to provide a steady population of prisoners to justify the expenditures on new prison construction. This means that the average citizen is much more vulnerable to experiencing a period of incarceration because the prisons must be filled to pay back both public and private investors, and this is particularly true in the southern and western states that have turned to private prisons since 1984 and today house approximately 8.4% of our total U.S. prison population (U.S. Department of Justice 2014). (For a brief history of America's Private Prison Industry, see Pauly 2016: http://www. motherjones.com/politics/2016/06/history-of-americas-private-prison-industry-timeline.)

Criminal justice scholars have compared the buildup of prisons in the United States to the **military industrial complex**, a term introduced to public discourse in 1961 by President Eisenhower in reference to an extreme preoccupation of the government with the buildup of the military, the production of weapons, and a consistent need to be engaged in war (Hattery and Smith 2010; Magnani 2011). Similarly, the phrase "**prison industrial complex**" has been used to describe the U.S. government's commitment to mass incarceration and new prison construction. So, if building up the military fuels the need for war, then building prisons fuels the need to increase the number of citizens who spend time in prison. It took some time for this to be recognized as a social problem and the recent recognition of the economic unsustainability of our prison system by individuals on both the left and the right of the political spectrum may lead to significant prison reform (Murphy 2014). Still, some segments of society still do not view this system as problematic and, in fact, consider a burgeoning prison system as good for the security and order of society (Enns 2014).

In Module 3, the impact of race on social status in the United States was examined. Beyond the recent and growing number of high profile cases that question police conduct in racial and ethnic minority communities, glaring racial disparities exist in the criminal justice system. While racial and ethnic minorities constitute approximately 30% of the total U.S. population, they account for 60% of the U. S. prison population (The Sentencing Project 2016). African American and Latino men in particular are significantly overrepresented in the U. S. prison population. African American men account for 50% of all imprisoned Americans and they have a one in three chance of spending time in jail at some point on their lifetime. At every stage of the criminal justice process, African American men are much more likely to become ensnared by the system. They are more likely to be arrested and their cases are more likely to proceed to a hearing, where ultimately they are more likely to be convicted (Smith and Hattery 2010; Elsner 2006). This has led to comparisons to the **penitentiary "farms" system** that came to fruition once slavery was abolished. African American men were routinely arrested for the smallest of transgressions and forced to work on plantations as "apprentices," immediately following the abolition of slavery.

The current politically correct environment makes it difficult to imprison racial minorities for trivial or trumped up charges. The reality is that crime rates are down, yet more and more people have become prisoners each year in the United States. How is this possible? The current mechanisms that promote the inflated rates of incarceration for racial and ethnic minorities are the sentencing guidelines and the "war on drugs" (Smith and Hattery 2010). Changes to sentencing guidelines such as mandatory minimum sentences and the "three strikes" or "habitual felon" laws, which allow judges to impose life sentences for individuals who receive a third felony conviction—regardless of the severity of the crime—have played in a significant role in the over-incarceration of racial and ethnic minorities. The reclassification of drug possession from a misdemeanor to a felony created criminals out of drug addicts, who many argue would be best served in medical treatment facilities (McVay, Schiraldi, and Ziedenberg 2004).

TABLE 14

Lifetime Likelihood of Imprisonment

White Men	1/17	White Women	1/211
Black Men	1/3	Black Women	1/18
Latino Men	1/6	Latina Women	1/45

The Sentencing Project 2016

Among the most controversial of the changes to sentencing laws—the disparate sentencing for crack versus powder cocaine—occurred when Congress passed the Anti-Drug Abuse Act of 1986. This law established mandatory minimum sentences for specific quantities of cocaine and the 100:1 sentencing ratio in which possession of 5 grams of crack or 500 grams of powder cocaine would result in a minimum five-year federal prison sentence. Despite the fact that no scientific evidence supports this sentencing disparity and the U.S. Sentencing Commission conclusion that "crack is not appreciably different from powder cocaine in either its chemical composition or the physical reactions of its users," Congress rejected the Commission's recommendation to revise the statutory penalties for crack cocaine (ACLU 2006). Racial disparity was embedded in the law, since African Americans are more frequently in the possession of crack cocaine and White Americans are more frequently in the possession of powder cocaine. In 2010, Congress finally heeded the Commission's recommendation and passed the Fair Sentencing Act (FSA) which "reduced the sentencing disparity between offenses for crack and powder cocaine from 100:1 to 18:1." In 2011, "the U. S. Sentencing Commission voted to retroactively apply the new FSA sentencing guidelines to individuals sentenced before the law was enacted...ensur[ing] that over 12,000 people—85% of whom are African Americans—will have the opportunity to have their sentences for crack cocaine offenses reviewed by a federal judge and possibly reduced" (ACLU 2016). Other similar reforms regarding drug sentencing laws are significant because two-thirds of all prisoners serving time for drug offenses are racial and ethnic minorities and 50% of the federal prisoners are imprisoned due to drug offenses.

The disparity in how racial and ethnic minorities are treated in the criminal justice system is problematic on its own, but the disparate rates of incarceration lead to a whole host of problems including difficulty finding employment, social disconnection from family, ineligibility for social welfare assistance, and political disenfranchisement in many states where individuals with a felony record are ineligible to vote (Roberts 2004; Smith and Hattery 2010). Pager's 2007 book *Marked*, discusses race, crime, and the challenges of finding work in an era of mass incarceration. The number of obstacles that must be overcome to successfully re-enter society after incarceration—particularly with regard to employment—makes ex-convicts vulnerable to returning to criminal activity. Currently, 75% of U.S. inmates are repeat offenders. This high rate of **recidivism** makes it necessary to ask whether the current U.S. criminal justice system is working and how re-entry to society could be structured to be more successful.

Combat Drones

Officially combat drones are referred to as **unmanned combat aerial vehicles** (UCAV). These aircraft do not have human pilots on board, but are under real-time human control. UCAVs are operated from remote terminals. Combat drones carry aircraft ordinance (e.g., bombs, missiles, rockets, gun ammunition, and/or surveillance equipment). Over 40 countries including China, France, India, Iran, Israel, Russia, Turkey, United Kingdom, and United States have drones with the capability to shoot laser-guided missiles ranging from 35–100 pounds (Reaching Critical Will 2016).

Many moral concerns exist regarding the use of UCAVs as they depersonalize violent acts and dehumanize war. Remotely attacking humans using missiles, artillery, and aerial bombs reduces casualties among attackers. Additionally, combat drones may be initiated autonomously to act

©Paul Fleet/Shutterstock.com

independently avoiding all direct human involvement, reducing human sensibility and awareness (Special Rapporteur 2012).

Several human rights groups argue combat drones do not accurately distinguish combatants from civilians resulting in collateral damage. Ross (2014) found from 2004 to 2012 there were 330 drone strikes in Pakistan, with approximately 2,479 to 3,180 people killed and over 1,000 injured, and 31 to 41 drone strikes in Yemen, with 317 to 826 people killed. Some scrutiny comes from the lack of transparency in data reported to the public about drone attacks and the number of civilian casualties. Because use of combat drones is "easy" and "risk-free," there is concern governments and military forces will broaden the interpretation of international humanitarian law to justify killing (Reaching Critical Will 2016).

With the military success of UCAVs, manufacturers expanded their markets to domestic surveillance and commercial use. With the convergence of other technologies, drones now are available to monitor individuals for profit-making ventures, pushing the boundaries of privacy laws. On June 21, 2016, the U.S. Federal Aviation Administration (FAA) opened pathways to integrate unmanned aircraft systems or drones into the nation's airspace. Under the auspices of safety and standards, the FAA requests operators to abide by *Voluntary Best Practices for UAS Privacy, Transparency, and Accountability* reiterating operators must abide by existing federal and state privacy laws (see the guide at: https://www.ntia.doc.gov/files/ntia/publications/voluntary_best_practices_for_uas_privacy_transparency_and_accountability_0.pdf).

Cybercrime

The development and integration of technology in society has created new types of crimes using the Internet and computer networks. **High-tech crimes** include cyber terrorism, espionage, computer intrusions, and fraud. The United States is the top country by victim location of cybercrime with California (34,832) and Florida (20,306) reporting the highest number of crimes (Internet Crime Complaint Center 2015). The U.S. Federal

Bureau of Investigations (FBI) created the Internet Crime Complaint Center (IC3) to receive complaints of Internet crime in an effort to mitigate economic loss by investigating and prosecuting offenders. In 2015, IC3 noted 127,145 complaints reported totaled over one trillion dollars in losses with the most prevalent types of cybercrimes in: 1) non-payment/non-delivery, 2) 419 money transfer/overpayment, 3) identity theft, and 4) auction (Internet Crime Complaint Center 2015).

Privacy

The infrastructure of the Internet and computer networks creates a challenge for protecting one's digital privacy. The diversity of technology and frequency of use by individuals and groups throughout the world make it difficult to create standards and laws to ensure confidentiality of personal information. Privacy is only protected as well as the cybersecurity employed, and its evident weaknesses of being physically and electronically isolated attract cybercriminals (Schell 2012). In 2015, 19,632 personal data breach complaints were filed with the FBI (Internet Crime Complaint Center 2015), not including other cybercrimes associated with stealing and using personal information, such as identity theft, extortion, credit card fraud, corporate data breach, health care related, etc.

The growth of technology and tech-based services has created a market economy based on the collection and sale of personal data (Ghernaouti-Hélie 2012). Not all organizations and businesses store and use personal data appropriately, ethically, or legally. It has become common practice for tech users to provide personal data, including tracking locator position, in exchange for services without even being aware or giving expressed, informed permission. Many large Internet service and social networking platform providers make large profits commercializing and exploiting personal data either given to them freely or, worse, without user knowledge (Ghernaouti-Hélie 2012). Additionally, all digital activities leave traces of personal data allowing permanent surveillance of users, violating their fundamental rights and civil liberties without consumer protection.

FIGURE 17

2015 Top 5 Countries by Victim Location

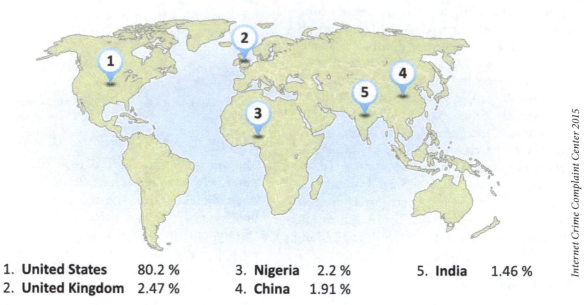

Internet Crime Complaint Center 2015

1. **United States** 80.2 %
2. **United Kingdom** 2.47 %
3. **Nigeria** 2.2 %
4. **China** 1.91 %
5. **India** 1.46 %

FIGURE 18

2015 Top 10 States by Victim Location

Internet Crime Complaint Center 2015

1. **California** 14.53 %
2. **Florida** 8.47 %
3. **Texas** 7.67 %
4. **New York** 6.30 %
5. **Illinois** 3.51 %
6. **Pennsylvania** 3.31 %
7. **Virginia** 3.14 %
8. **New Jersey** 3.01 %
9. **Washington** 2.72 %
10. **Ohio** 2.69 %

TABLE 15

2015 Crime Types

Crime Type	Victim Count	Crime Type	Victim Count
Non-Payment/Non-Delivery	67,375	Lottery/Sweepstakes	5,324
419/Overpayment	30,855	Malware/Scareware	3,294
Identity Theft	21,949	Corporate Data Breach	2,499
Auction	21,510	Ransomware	2,453
Other	19,963	IPR/Copyright and Counterfeit	1,931
Personal Data Breach	19,632	Investment	1,806
Employment	18,758	Crimes against Children	1,348
Extortion	17,804	Civil Matter	1,148
Credit Card Fraud	17,172	Re-shipping	1,073
Phishing/Vishing/Smishing/Pharming	16,594	Denial of Service	1,020
Advanced Fee	16,445	Virus	971
Harassment/Threats of Violence	14,812	Health Care Related	465
Confidence Fraud/Romance	12,509	Charity	411
No Lead Value	12,187	Terrorism	361
Government Impersonation	11,832	Hacktivist	211
Real Estate/Rental	11,562	Gambling	131
Business Email Compromise	7,837	Criminal Forums	62
Misrepresentation	5,458		
Descriptors*			
Social Media	19,967		
Virtual Currency	1,920		

*These descriptors are used by the IC3 for tracking purposes only and are only available after another crime type has been selected.

Internet Crime Complaint Center 2015

Identity Theft and Fraud

Identity theft and fraud refer to crimes in which someone wrongfully obtains and uses another person's personal data in a deceptive way for economic gain (U.S. Department of Justice 2015). Social security, bank account, and credit card numbers and other identifying data have been stolen by unauthorized persons to withdraw funds from accounts, incur debts, file taxes, and commit crimes in victims' names. According to the U.S. Department of Justice 21,949 individuals were victims of identity theft in the United States in 2015.

INTERNET SCAMMING IN GHANA

Internet scams originating from Ghana are typically unsolicited communications either inviting investors to participate in a quick financial gain opportunity or friend/love requests that will eventually lead to asking for funds to travel or pay for living/medical expenses. Click on the link below to learn more about Internet scamming in Ghana: https://youtu.be/o26Eks801oc

The most common ways to commit identity theft or fraud is by "shoulder surfing" (watching or listening to people using their information), stealing information from someone's mailboxes or trash, and spam or sending unsolicited emails requesting data in exchange for a benefit (U.S. Department of Justice 2015). In Ghana, West Africa, unemployed men and boys are becoming Internet gangsters practicing *Sakawa* or Internet fraud and witchcraft. These Gangsters use spam to lure potential identity theft and fraud victims throughout the world. *Sakawa* has become normalized in West Africa and is viewed as an upstanding career in some cultures.

Cyberbullying

Technology and the Internet have changed how people interact with each other. People are no longer required to verbally or physically confront each other to communicate. Advances in technology and the Internet provide a platform for people to be anonymous or someone else and treat others in ways that would not be considered acceptable or normal if communicated verbally or in a face-to-face setting.

Technology and the Internet have created a new venue for bullying. A **cyberbully** uses technological communications to threaten, harass, or intimidate others. According to Anderson, Bresnahan, and Musatics (2014) cyberbullying lowers self-esteem, increases depression, and increases

Sociological Application 5.5

The Impact of Cyberbullying

Watch a clip on cyberbullying from the film *This Emotional Life* at https://youtu.be/jpBZIXvEYsU.

1. What are popular methods of cyberbullying? What impact do these methods have on the emotional state of victims?

2. Have you experienced or know someone who has experienced in-person bullying or cyberbullying? Were you a bully? What effect did the bullying have on the victim?

3. Examine the demographics of youth who experienced cyberbullying during the 2012–2013 school year: http://nces.ed.gov/pubs2015/2015056.pdf. Based on the statistics, who do you think is most likely to be a target of cyberbullying? Why?

4. What is being done to reduce the incidence of cyberbullying among school-age youth? Why is it hard to eliminate this form of bullying? What do you think might be an effective solution?

feelings of powerlessness among victims. Approximately 6.9% or 1,713,000 students experienced cyberbullying during the 2012–2013 school year (National Center for Education Statistics 2013). Homosexual and bisexual teens report a higher frequency of cyberbullying than heterosexual teens (Statistic Brain 2016).

Cyberbullying is prevalent on social media sites. Approximately 84.2% of cyberbullying incidents reported occurred on Facebook, 23.4% on Instagram, 21.4% on Twitter, 13.5% on Snap Chat, and 11.2% using Instant Messages (Statistic Brain 2016). Mitchell, Jones, Turner, and Wolak (2015) found mixed harassment incidents involving

TABLE 16

Students 12–18 Years Old Who Reported Being Bullied at School and Cyber-bullied Anywhere in 2012–2013		
Type of Bullying	Number of Students	Percent of Students
Total bullied or not bullied	25,013,000	100.0
Bullied	5,386,000	21.5
Made fun of, called names, or insulted	3,410,000	13.6
Subject of rumors	3,295,000	13.2
Threatened with harm	979,000	3.9
Pushed, shoved, tripped, or spit on	1,509,000	6.0
Tried to make do things they did not want to do	548,000	2.2
Excluded from activities on purpose	1,114,000	4.5
Property destroyed on purpose	390,000	1.6
Not bullied	19,627,000	78.5
Total cyber-bullied or not cyber-bullied	24,985,000	100.0
Cyber-bullied	1,713,000	6.9
Hurtful information on Internet	705,000	2.8
Purposely shared private information	230,000	0.9
Unwanted contact via e-mail	236,000	0.9
Unwanted contact via instant messaging	532,000	2.1
Unwanted contact via text messaging	796,000	3.2
Unwanted contact via online gaming	373,000	1.5
Purposeful exclusion from an online community	228,800	0.9
Not cyber-bullied	23,272,000	93.1

Source: U.S. Department of Justice, Bureau of Justice Statistics, School Crime Supplement (SCS) to the National Crime Victimization Survey (NCVS), 2013.

http://citylimits.org/2012/08/24/beyond-the-nra-pro-gun-groups-arent-in-lock-step/

both in-person and online bullying have the most emotional distressing impact on victims and to involve perpetrator(s) who had deeper relationships to the victim. These incidences were reported as having the most impact on victims because perpetrators shared victims' personal information on social media sites. Research shows cyberbullying has the greatest influence on individuals experiencing victimization across multiple areas of their lives (Mitchell et al. 2015).

Evaluating Critical Thinking and Credibility

This module provides us with a realistic understanding about issues related to crime and violence. Because crime and violence are often associated with heinous acts our intuition inflates our perceptions about the frequency of violence against persons re-enforcing the fear of crime. Our fears then exaggerate our prejudices towards people who we correlate and stereotype in relation to certain types of crimes.

1. Consider the different social issues presented in this module.
2. Describe how ideological and empirical reasoning might influence people's perceptions about crime and violence.
3. Discuss any fallacies you discovered in your thinking about the issues presented and specify which of your assumptions were challenged.
4. Explore which crimes and violent acts you associate with particular types of people (e.g., age, gender, race, social class, etc.) and explain how context changes your perspective about these groups (e.g., Muslims on a plane vs. Muslims in a Mosque).

Theoretical Analysis

In applying functionalism to the examination of deviance, three different perspectives may be invoked. One perspective is strain theory. **Functionalism** examines deviance and how

people challenge and break norms (both formal and informal rules) and set boundaries around norms. **Strain theory** observes how people rationalize rule breaking when they are unable to legitimately obtain or meet goals. For example, if I lose my job and I'm unable to pay my mortgage or feed my children and there are no job opportunities in my community, I will begin to develop stress and anxiety and begin considering desperate measures to survive (e.g., robbery, prostitution, gambling, etc.). People face societal pressure because they are unable to cope or survive within the norm, so they seek illegitimate means to obtain the desired ends.

The second functionalist perspective is called social disorganization theory. **Social disorganization theory** examines how the structure of the social environment inhibits people from social and economic prospects leading to success. In other words, if I live in an impoverished community with limited educational opportunities, primarily minimum wage jobs, inadequate or substandard housing, and limited public transportation infrastructure, then I am unable to have the chance to improve my social and economic mobility or social class. Thus, the social environment influences deviant or rule breaking behavior because people do not have access to the structural supports they need to survive and become successful.

Social disorganization theory is related to **cultural deviance theory**, another functionalist perspective. The lack of resources in poor communities creates a culture outside the norms of accepted methods for achieving social and

©Romariolen/Shutterstock.com

economic success. Impoverished communities develop their own cultural norms or rules differently than mainstream society to accommodate or fit their surroundings and lack of resources. In communities with limited and low paying jobs, alternative methods for generating become acceptable for obtaining income (e.g., prostitution, selling drugs, etc.).

When applied to deviance, **conflict theory** studies how the unequal distribution of resources influences the treatment of people around rules and rule breaking. People with resources create the laws that govern society, which means they hold the power to create laws that provide them opportunities to obtain and sustain their power and freedom. People with power and wealth often go under-punished for the crimes they commit. For the same reason they are able to create laws, money gives them the access to defense attorneys but also influence on the judicial system.

Interactionism examines symbols and words to understand the interpretation and meaning of interactions. With regard to deviance, interactionists look at how people perceive and apply meaning to deviant behavior. Three different perspectives categorized under interactionism and be used to examine deviant behavior.

The first interactionist perspective is **labeling theory**. People use labels to identify rule breakers or norm violators. Some commonly used labels are "delinquent," "criminal," "crazy," etc. Labels have

©IvanNikulin/Shutterstock.com

a social and psychological influence on people. When a label is consistently applied in the social environment to an individual, the person often begins to behave in a manner fitting the label. The more we use a label on someone, the more they accept it as "real," and start acting out the behavior associated with the label. So, if we call young people who act out at school trouble makers and delinquent, tell them they are not going to amount to anything, they are no good, and use derogatory terms to address them (e.g., loser, stupid, idiot, etc.), they will likely begin to believe the labels, exhibit behavior expected of the labels, and fulfill the prophecy of the labels.

The second interactionist perspective is called **differential association**. This perspective looks at how people learn rule breaking behavior from associates or through group learning. In other words, the people we associate with socialize us. So, if someone grows up in an environment where their parents are gang members, that person is socialized around gang culture, ideals, and rules or norms and is more likely to think and act in ways associated with that culture.

The last interactionist perspective is called **control theory**. People take cues from social controls with others to help guide thinking and behavior. Social controls influence thinking and behavior because of the social bonds people create and expect from each other. This is why everyone stands in line in social settings because we are concerned about the social consequences or breaking the social bond by violating the rule. When limited or no social bonds exist, people do not feel obligated to abide by norms or rules. For example, if class ends and someone leaves a backpack on a desk and only one person is left in the room, the remaining student has ample opportunity rummage through the backpack, take the bag or other item left inside, or do nothing and leave the room without feeling responsible or getting caught for their actions. Without any social bonds to others, no social controls confine our behavior.

In applying the feminist paradigm to the study of deviant behavior, theorists observe the lives and experiences of women and minorities in the creation and implementation of formal and informal rules. **Feminism** analyzes the differences in the treatment of women and minorities including violation of human rights upheld by laws and societal norms. This paradigm assesses how the rules of oppression are sustained and re-enforced in society.

Exchange theorists investigate the motives behind rule-breaking behavior. An assessment of motives helps us understand how people evaluate and analyze the risks and gains for defying the rules. This paradigm also helps reveal personal and social influences of deviant behavior.

Lastly, **environmental theory** surveys the development of norms or rules and the laws to enforce social control. This paradigm examines how social problems have historically been addressed in social, political, economic, and legal arenas. In the application of deviant behavior, environmental theory considers the adaptation of deviant behavior over time and the changing context of acceptable norms in the creation and development of formal rules, policies, and laws.

As we use theoretical paradigms to examine the social world, we must be mindful of how each theory focuses on a particular level of analysis. Combined, the six paradigms offer a comprehensive understanding of social structure. Individually, each paradigm provides insight into the influence of the social world on thinking and behavior and vice versa. The theories help enhance critical thought by making us analyze and evaluate the social world from different levels of analysis to develop a comprehensive understanding of the human condition and the social issues we face.

©trekandshoot/Shutterstock.com

Choose one of the following social problems and explain the issue and its impact on society:

- Declaration of war and authorized use of military force
- Terrorism
- Genocide
- Elite deviance
- Prison industrial complex
- Drones
- Mass shootings
- Infanticide
- Executions
- Forced labor
- Sex trafficking
- Privacy
- Identity theft and fraud
- Cyberbullying

Analyze the problem using the six theoretical paradigms. Provide specific examples from this module to justify your analysis.

- Functionalism
  - Strain theory
  - Social disorganization theory
  - Cultural deviance theory
- Conflict theory
- Interactionism
  - Labeling theory
  - Differential association theory
  - Control theory
- Feminism
- Exchange theory
- Environmental theory

Social Policy

Students have a long history of leading social change and pushing new policy development. Watch *Education for Social Change* by Artika R. Tyner (https://www.youtube.com/watch?v=P5QHAhMYwoA) to learn how students have worked together to address social policy issues like those presented in this module.

1. Explain how you would organize a movement to change a policy or law addressing one of the social issues presented in this module.
2. Discuss your message or proposed law and how you would create awareness about the policy or law you want to change/develop.
3. Describe how you would recruit people to join your movement and donate their time and money to creating social change.
4. Explain your strategy for influencing political leaders to adopt and sponsor your proposed bill.

Social Movements and Reform

Any discussion about social problems ought to include a conversation about solutions. Each of the social issues presented in this module have a

©Victor Brave/Shutterstock.com

variety of groups working to change, reform, or address the problem. The success of any social transformation depends on the unity, resources, and persistence of the social group working towards change. Successful social movements require a structure and organization to ensure the group's message is clear, membership is developed, and financial and other resources are garnered to sustain operations. A conducive political environment and good timing can also make a movement more successful.

Each of the following groups is working toward social transformation on some of the issues presented in this module.

- The Non-Violence Project (http://www.non-violence.com/about/the-foundation/)
- Walk Free (http://www.walkfree.org/)
- Stomp Out Bullying (http://www.stompout-bullying.org/)

Research and investigate these organizations to assess the impact they are having on the social issue they are addressing.

1. What is the mission/goal of the organization?
2. What is the history of the organization? When was it founded?
3. How many members are involved in each organization?
4. What is the process for joining the organization and/or volunteering?
5. What support does the organization receive (e.g., grants, donations, volunteers, etc.)?
6. Who provides financial and other support to the organization?
7. What success in social transformation or changing social policy has the organization demonstrated to date? Explain the group's achievements and/or challenges to success.
8. Identify any groups or movements in your community addressing the social problems presented in this module.

References

American Civil Liberties Union. 2006. "Cracks in the System: Twenty Years of the Unjust Federal Crack Cocaine Law." Retrieved February 25, 2016 (https://www.aclu.org/sites/default/files/field_document/cracksinsystem_20061025.pdf).

American Civil Liberties Union. 2016. "Fair Sentencing Act." Retrieved February 25, 2016 (https://www.aclu.org/feature/fair-sentencing-act).

Anderson, Jenn, Mary Bresnahan, and Catherine Musatics. 2014. "Combating Weight-Based Cyberbullying on Facebook with the Dissenter Effect." *Cyberpsychology, Behavior, and Social Networkin* 17(5):281–286.

Auron, Yair. 2004. *The Banality of Denial: Israel and the Armenian Genocide.* New Brunswick, NJ Transaction Publishers.

Bales, Kevin. 2002. "The Social Psychology of Modern Slavery." *Scientific American, Inc.,* April 24, pp. 1–4.

Bureau of Justice Statistics. 2014. "The Nation's Two Measures of Homicide." NCJ 247060. Office of Justice Programs. Washington, D.C.: U.S. Department of Justice.

Congressional Research Service. 2014. *Declarations of War and Authorizations for the Use of Military Force: Historical Background and Legal Implications.* Washington, DC: Library of Congress.

Curra, John. 2014. *The Relativity of Deviance.* 3rd ed. Thousand Oaks, CA: Sage.

Death Penalty Information Center (DPIC). 2016. "Facts about the Death Penalty." Retrieved June 27, 2016 (http://www.deathpenaltyinfo.org/documents/FactSheet.pdf).

Declercq, Frederic and Kurt Audenaert. 2011. "Predatory Violence Aiming at Relief in a Case of Mass Murder: Meloy's Criteria for Applied Forensic Practice." *Behavioral Sciences and the Law* 29(4): http://citylimits.org/2012/08/24/beyond-the-nra-pro-gun-groups-arent-in-lock-step/578–591.

Domhoff, G. William. 1998. *Who Rules America?* New York: McGraw-Hill.

Elsner, Alan. 2006. *Gates of Injustice: The Crisis in America's Prisons.* New York: Prentice Hall.

Enns, Peter. 2014. "The Public's Increasing Punitiveness and Its Increasing Influence on Mass Incarceration in the United States." *American Journal of Political Science* 58 (4): 857–872.

Fisher, Max. 2013. "This Map Shows Where the World's 30 Million Slaves Live. There are 60,000 in the U.S." *The Washington Post,* October 17.

Friedrichs, David O. 2002. "Occupational Crime, Occupational Deviance, and Workplace Crime: Sorting Out the Difference." *Criminology and Criminal Justice* 2(3):243–256.

Gettings, John and Catherine McNiff. 2000 – 2016. "Milestones in Federal Gun Control Legislation." Infoplease. Sandbox Networks, Inc., publishing as Infoplease. Retrieved June 26, 2016 (http://www.infoplease.com/spot/guntime1.html).

Ghernaouti-Hélie, Solange. 2012. "The Cybercrime Ecosystem & Privacy Issues Main Challenges and Perspectives from a Societal Perspective." *ERCIM News* 90:1–60.

Gun Violence Archive. 2016. "Mass Shootings." Retrieved June 26, 2016 (http://www.shooting-tracker.com/).

Hanlon, Robert E., Michael Brook, John Stratton, Marie Jensen, and Leah H Rubin. 2013. Neuropsychological and intellectual differences between types of murderers: Affective/impulsive versus predatory/instrumental (premeditated) homicide. *Criminal Justice and Behavior,* 40(3), 933–948.

Hattery, Angela and Earl Smith. 2008. "A Tool for Racial Segregation and Labor Exploitation." *Race, Gender, and Class* 15:79–97.

Herman, Edward S. 1986. "Power and the Semantics of Terrorism." Covert Action Quarterly 26:9–16.

Internet Crime Complaint Center. 2015. "2015 Internet Crime Report." Federal Bureau of Investigation. Washington, DC: U.S. Department of Justice.

Knafo, Saki. 2013. "Prison-Industrial Complex? Maybe it's Time for A Schools-Industrial Complex." Huffingtonpost.com, August 31. Retrieved June 25, 2016 (http://www.huffingtonpost.com/2013/08/30/california-prisons-schools_n_3839190.html).

Kotrla, Kimberly. 2010. "Domestic Minor Sex Trafficking in the United States." *Social Work* 55(2):181–187.

Lankford, Adam. 2016. "Public Mass Shooters and Firearms: Cross-National Study of 171 Countries." *Violence and Victims.* 31(2): 187–99. Retrieved June 26, 2016 (http://www.ncbi.nlm.nih.gov/pubmed/26822013).

Magnani, Laura. 2011. "Market Values Permeate Both Foreign Policies and Prison Policies." *Peace Review* 23(3):279–286.

Markon, Jerry and Robert Frank. 2002. "Adelphia Officials Are Arrested, Charged With Massive Fraud." *The Wall Street Journal.* Retrieved June 29, 2016 (http://www.wsj.com/articles/SB1027516262583067680).

McVay, Doug, Vincent Schiraldi, and Jason Ziedenberg. 2004. "Treatment or Incarceration? National and State Findings on the Efficacy and Cost Savings of Drug Treatment versus Imprisonment." Policy Report. Washington, DC: Justice Policy Institute.

Meloy, J. Reid. 2006. "Empirical Basis and Forensic Application of Affective and Predatory Violence." *Australian and New Zealand Journal of Psychiatry* 40(6–7):539–547.

Mills, C. Wright. 1956. *The Power Elite.* New York: Oxford University Press.

Mitchell, Kimberly J., Lisa M. Jones, Heather A. Turner, and Janis Wolak. 2015. *Technology-Involved Harassment Victimization: Placement in a Broader Victimization Context.* NIJ Grant No. 2012-IJ-CX-0024. Washington, DC: U.S. Department of Justice.

Moran, Dianne. 2003. "Infanticide." Macmillan Encyclopedia of Death and Dying. Farmington Hills, Michigan: Gale Group, Inc. Retrieved June 27, 2016 (http://www.encyclopedia.com/topic/infanticide.aspx).

Murphy, Carla. 2014. "A New Development in Prison Reform." Colorlines.com, January 30. Retrieved June 25, 2016 (http://www.colorlines.com/articles/new-development-prison-reform).

Murphy, Jarrett. 2012. "Beyond the NRA: Pro-gun Groups aren't in Lock Step." CityLimits.org. Retrieved on June 30, 2016 (http://citylimits.org/2012/08/24/beyond-the-nra-pro-gun-groups-arent-in-lock-step/).

National Center for Education Statistics. 2013. "Student Reports of Bullying and Cyberbullying: Results from the 2013 School Crime Supplement to the National Crime Victimization Survey." NCES 2015-056. Washington, DC: U.S. Department of Education.

Ooten, Melissa. 2010. "Tackling the PIC: Successes and Challenges in Teaching the Prison- Industrial Complex." *Radical Teacher* 88:32–42.

Owens, Colleen, Meredith Dank, Justin Breaux, Isela Banuelos, Amy Farrell, Rebecca Pfeffer, Katie Bright, Ryan Heitsmith, and Jack McDevitt. 2015. "Understanding the Organization, Operation, and Victimization Process of Labor Trafficking in the United States." *Trends in Organized Crime* 18:348–354.

New America. 2016. "Deadly Attacks since 9/11." Retrieved June 22, 2016 (http://securitydata.newamerica.net/extremists/deadly-attacks.html).

Pager, Devah. 2007. *Marked: Race, Crime, and Finding Work in an Era of Mass Incarceration*. Chicago, IL: University of Chicago Press.

Pauly, Madison. 2016. "A Brief History of America's Private Prison Industry. MotherJones. com, July/August 2016. Retrieved June 25, 2016 (http://www.motherjones.com/politics/2016/06/history-of-americas-private-prison-industry-timeline).

Peters, Alicia W. 2013. "Things that Involve Sex are Just Different: US Anti-Trafficking law and Policy on the Books, in Their Minds, and in Action." *Anthropological Quarterly* 86(1):221–256.

Pinheiro, Paulo Sergio. 2006. *World Report on Violence against Children*. New York: United Nations.

Reaching Critical Will. 2016. "Drones." New York: Women's International League for Peace and Freedom.

Roberts, Dorothy E. 2004. "The Social and Moral Cost of Mass Incarceration in African American Communities." *Stanford Law Review* 56(5):1271–1305.

Ross, Alice K. 2014. "Get the Data: Drone Wars." London: Bureau of Investigative Journalism.

Schell, Roger R. 2012. "Current Cybersecurity Best Practice—a Clear and Present Danger to Privacy." *ERCIM News* 90:1–60.

Sentencing Project. 2016. "Racial Disparity." Retrieved June 25, 2016 (http://www.sentencingproject.org/issues/racial-disparity/).

Smith, Earl and Angela Hattery. 2006. "If We Build It They Will Come: Human Rights Violations and the Prison Industrial Complex." *Society without Borders* 2(2):276–292.

Smith, Earl and Angela Hattery. 2010. "African American Men and the Prison Industrial Complex." *The Western Journal of Black Studies* 34(2):387–398.

Special Rapporteur. 2014. "Report of the Special Rapporteur on the promotion and protection of human rights and fundamental freedoms while countering terrorism, Ben Emmerson." A/HRC/25/59. New York: Office of the United Nations High Commissioner for Human Rights.

Spitzer, Eliot. 2009. "The Real AIG Scandal." *Slate. com*. Retrieved June 29, 2016 (http://www.slate.com/articles/news_and_politics/the_best_policy/2009/03/the_real_aig_scandal.html).

Staff writer. 2002. "Enron: The Real Scandal." *The Economist*. Retrieved June 29, 2016 (http://www.economist.com/node/940091).

Statistic Brain. 2016. "Cyberbullying/Bullying Statistics." Retrieved June 23, 2016 (http://www.statisticbrain.com/cyber-bullying-statistics/).

U.S. Department of Justice. 2014. "Prisoners in 2013." Retrieved June 25, 2016 (http://www.bjs.gov/content/pub/pdf/p13.pdf).

U.S. Department of Justice. 2015. "Identity Theft." Retrieved June 23, 2016 (https://www.justice.gov/criminal-fraud/identity-theft/identity-theft-and-identity-fraud).

United States Holocaust Memorial Museum. 2016. "Holocaust Encyclopedia" Retrieved June 22, 2016 (https://www.ushmm.org/wlc/en/article.php?ModuleId=10007043).

Willingham, AJ. 2016. "U.S. Home to Nearly a Third of World's Mass Shootings." CNN. Retrieved June 26, 2016 (http://www.cnn.com/2016/06/13/health/mass-shootings-in-america-in-charts-and-graphs-trnd/).

Winslow, Robert W. and Sheldon X. Zhang. 2008. *Criminology: A Global Perspective*. Upper Saddle River, NJ: Prentice Hall.

Yang, Stephanie. 2014. "5 Years Ago Bernie Madoff Was Sentenced to 150 Years in Prison—Here's How His Scheme Worked." *Business Insider*. Retrieved June 29, 2016 (http://www.businessinsider.com/how-bernie-madoffs-ponzi-scheme-worked-2014-7).

Zimmer, Teresa A., Johnathan Sheldon, David A. Lubarsky, Francisco Lopez-Munoz, Linda Waterman, Richard Weisman, Leonidas G. Koniaris. 2007. "Lethal Injection for Execution: Chemical Asphyxiation?" *PLoS Med* 4(4):1–6. Retrieved June 29, 2016 (http://www.medscape.com/viewarticle/556167_4).

Do you know the terms?

Using the list provided below, create a personal dictionary of key terms and concepts presented in this module. Include the term, phonetic spelling (if needed), and definition in your own words. Next, provide a real world example of the term or concept based on your previous knowledge or new information you learned in this module to help re-enforce learning.

Absolute or moralistic perspective

Conflict theory

Control theory

Cultural deviance theory

Cyberbullying

Cybercrime

Declaration of war

Deviance

Differential association

Elite deviance

Environmental theory

Exchange theory

Executions

Feminism

Forced labor

Forced prostitution

Genocide

Gun control

Identity theft and fraud

Infanticide

Labeling theory

Mass shootings

Medical/social-pathological perspective

Military-industrial complex

Modern slavery

Norms

Organizational deviance

Penitentiary "farms" system

Power elite

Predatory violence

Prison industrial complex

Relativistic perspective

Sanctions

Sex trafficking

Social control

Social disorganization theory

State violence

Strain theory

Terrorism

Unmanned combat aerial vehicles

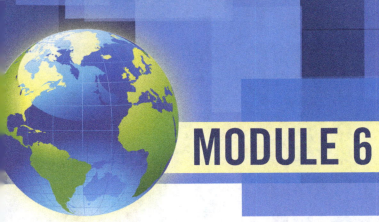

MODULE 6

Physical, Mental, and Social Wellness

Defining Health Disparities and Inequalities

In Module 3, the impact of economic inequality was examined. One consequence of having inadequate financial resources is the inability to access quality health care, which translates into increased vulnerability to disparities in health outcomes. Health disparities or inequalities are gaps in health outcomes or determinants among segments of the population. Aside from economic inequality, a number of social, environmental, and demographic factors contribute to health disparities.

It is quite challenging to attain optimal health outcomes without access to quality health care. In the United States, despite recent efforts to expand health care coverage through the Affordable Care Act (ACA), roughly 17% of the population remains uninsured and another sizable proportion (22%) of U.S. citizens are underinsured (Gold 2009; Commonwealth Fund 2015). Even with health care coverage, many people struggle to pay for expensive medical treatments. Individuals without health insurance are almost three times as likely to be without a primary care provider (57.9%) as individuals with private (19.5%) or public insurance (18.1%). Having a primary care provider is associated with higher levels of trust in medical practitioners and a greater probability of patients receiving high quality care (www.HealthyPeople.gov).

©Ricardo Reitmeyer/Shutterstock.com

In developed (high-income) countries such as the United States, acute diseases such as malaria, diarrhea, and measles no longer pose a threat, because resources such as water, adequate medical treatments, and sanitation services are available to help manage and control such diseases. Developing (middle-income) countries and especially less developed (low-income) countries, experience high rates of morbidity and mortality due to acute diseases. Diarrhea remains a leading cause of mortality among children under five years of age in low- and middle-income countries "due to inadequate water and sanitation and nutritional risk factors, such as suboptimal breastfeeding and zinc and vitamin A deficiency" (Fischer Walker, Perin, Aryee, Boschi-Pinto, and Black 2012). In contrast, in high-income countries, chronic diseases, such as diabetes, cancer, heart disease and obesity pose the greatest health threat. Some of these conditions are considered "luxury" or "fat cat" diseases, because lifestyle choices, such as smoking, excessive alcohol intake, drug dependency, poor diet, and physical inactivity, play a significant role in contraction.

Morbidity, mortality, and life expectancy data provide the best overview of any nation's health. **Morbidity** data captures the incidence and prevalence of diseases, the symptoms associated with diseases, and the resulting incapacities or impairments produced by the ailments. Incidence is the number of new cases of a disease, while prevalence is the total number of cases of a disease present in a given population at any one time. **Mortality** data measures death rates across various populations and the factors resulting in death. By examining morbidity and mortality data, life expectancy, or the number of years on average that a person born in a certain year can expect to live, can be calculated. Average **life expectancy** varies considerably from country to country with high-income countries experiencing much longer average life spans and low-income countries experiencing much shorter average life spans (CDC 2013).

Social Issues

Obesity

Being **overweight** means an individual has excess body weight that may be due to muscle, bone, fat, or water composition. **Obese** individuals have excess body fat. Two-thirds of the U.S. population is considered overweight or obese and more than a third (34.9%) of all U.S. adults are obese. About 5% of the population is extremely obese. Children are also finding it challenging to maintain a healthy weight with a third of children and adolescents being overweight or obese and 17% of children falling into the obese category (CDC 2015).

Body mass index (BMI) is the most common way of measuring overweight and obesity. According to the World Health Organization ("Obesity and Overweight" 2015), BMI is defined as a person's weight in kilograms divided by the square of [person's] height in meters (kg/m²)." A BMI greater

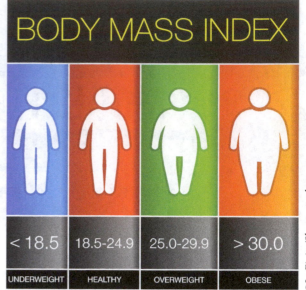

BODY MASS INDEX

| < 18.5 | 18.5-24.9 | 25.0-29.9 | > 30.0 |
| UNDERWEIGHT | HEALTHY | OVERWEIGHT | OBESE |

©In-Finity/Shutterstock.com

than or equal to 25 is overweight. Greater than or equal to 30 is obesity. Racial and ethnic variations exist in the extent of overweight and obesity. Roughly 75% of African Americans/Blacks and Hispanics/Latinos are overweight or obese compared to 67% of whites. Almost half of African Americans/Blacks and 39% of Latinos/Hispanics are obese compared to a third (34.3%) of whites. Blacks (13.1%) are more than twice as likely as whites (5.7%) or Latinos (5%) to be extremely obese. Asian Americans have very low rates of obesity (10.8%). Some studies, though, suggest BMI is not a good assessment of overweight or obesity for all racial and ethnic groups (NIDDK 2012; CDC 2015).

Measuring obesity is important because it is the gateway disease to chronic diseases such as type 2 diabetes, stroke, certain forms of cancer, osteoarthritis, high blood pressure, nonalcoholic fatty liver disease, and heart disease. Understanding what causes weight gain is simple. The science is clear. Weight gain results when there is an energy imbalance. When more energy is consumed in the form of food and drink than is burned in the form of activity, then weight gain will result.

Many factors contribute to obesity. Some individuals are genetically predisposed to be overweight or obese. Others have medical conditions that make it difficult to maintain a healthy weight.

In both cases, being overweight or obese is not inevitable, but it will require tremendous efforts to beat the odds. The effort to avoid being overweight or obese entails making healthy lifestyle choices such as eating a nutritious and balanced diet, exercising, managing stress and emotions, and abstaining from smoking, using drugs, and excessive drinking. Other factors that influence weight include environment and income (NIDDK 2012). Low-income women have higher rates of obesity than high-income women (CDC 2015); however, the reverse is true for men. High-income men experience greater rates of obesity than low-income men. Both of these are related to an important social issue discussed in Module 3, **food deserts**. People living in low-income neighborhoods and communities tend to have limited access to fresh fruits and vegetables, grains, and lean meats in inadequately-stocked corner stores, as full-fledged grocery stores are much less common in these communities. Residents of these neighborhoods are more likely to find processed foods high in calories, but low in nutrients. Eating these types of foods consistently over time makes people vulnerable to obesity and many of the other "luxury" diseases.

Tobacco

In 1965, Congress passed the Cigarette Labeling and Advertising Act which mandated that every pack of cigarettes have a label on its side with the warning "Cigarettes may be hazardous to your health." The fact that the law only mandated that the labels indicate that cigarettes might by dangerous can be attributed to political power that the companies in the tobacco industry wield. The primary ingredient in cigarettes is tobacco. More than 4000 chemicals are in cigarettes and the smoke they produce, including nicotine—a highly addictive stimulant that speeds up the nervous system, making the heart beat faster and increasing blood pressure. At least 51 of the chemicals found in cigarettes are known carcinogens, which cause cancer. Smoking cigarettes also causes heart disease, leads to heart attacks and stroke, and is associated with other diseases such as the flu and pneumonia (Jacobs 1995). There is

©Krunja/Shutterstock.com

no doubt that cigarettes are a health hazard and there never was. The tobacco industry also exacts a great toll on the environment (Madeley 1999).

Although the rate of smoking has declined over the last decade, still about 17% (40 million people) of the adult U.S. population smokes. About 16 million adults live with a smoking related disease. Cigarette smoking accounts for one of every five deaths in the United States, making cigarette smoking the leading cause of preventable deaths in the United States (CDC 2016). Most cigarette smokers start smoking before the age of 18. This fact is not lost on the tobacco industry, which targets the youth market with flavored tobacco products appealing to this demographic group. The rate of smoking traditional cigarettes is down among teenagers, but the use of electronic cigarettes and other tobacco delivery methods is increasing. In 2015, about 25% of high school students and 7% of middle school students used some form of tobacco (CDC 2016).

The tobacco industry has been always been an integral part of the United States economy because it has always produced reliable profits since it maintains a trade surplus meaning that it exports more than it imports. The tobacco industry is able to maintain such high profit margins because tobacco is a cheap crop to grow and human capital costs are low because cigarettes are manufactured by machines. Continued efforts to educate the public on the dangers of cigarette smoking and the growing number of communities that have adopted no smoking ordinances for public places, has put a dent in the U.S. tobacco market. As more and more legislation was passed to regulate the marketing, selling and use of cigarettes and other tobacco products, major U.S tobacco companies (Philip Morris USA/Altria Group, RJ Reynolds, American Brands) have been able to expand their economic base by purchasing companies outside of the tobacco industry and by selling their tobacco products in hundreds of countries around the world. They have also used their considerable economic power to lobby lawmakers to continue to provide them with favorable farming policies. Tobacco companies have also been able to maintain their status and power by reinvesting their profits into highly influential and some would argue manipulative advertisements (WHO 2013).

Big Pharma

Big Pharma is the term used to refer to the pharmaceutical industry and its trade group, Pharmaceutical Research and Manufacturers of America (PhRMA). It controls the distribution of prescription drugs and medical devices. In 2014, pharmaceutical sales around the world totaled over one trillion dollars and almost half of that was generated by the top 10 pharmaceutical companies. Five of the top 10 pharmaceutical companies are based in the United States. Big Pharma has been able to use its economic power to access political power. Over the last 16 years, the pharmaceutical industry has spent about three billion dollars on lobbying expenses. This is in addition to the millions of dollars that the industry has donated to fund the political campaigns of various candidates. They also make a deliberate effort to hire former government workers, particularly those with significant political capital (Drugwatch 2016).

The industry's strongest tool for maintaining power and authority over the distribution of prescription drugs and medical devices is the billions of dollars that it spends on advertising. Pharmaceutical companies spend 19 times as much on advertising as they do on research. These ads very skillfully manipulate the public into thinking that they will be better off if they use the drugs

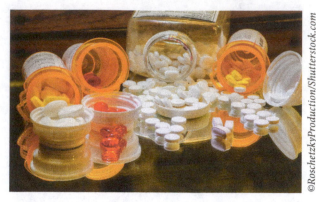

©RoschetzkyProduction/Shutterstock.com

being advertised. Only two countries, the United States and Switzerland, allow pharmaceutical companies to advertise their drugs directly to the public (Drugwatch 2016).

Doctors, scientists, and researchers are influenced by the large sums of money that pharmaceuticals can donate to their research or clinical trials. The industry engages in ghostwriting, or paying physicians to attach their names to articles that provide positive reviews of particular drugs with the hope of seeing the article published in a high-profile medical journal. The reality is that these articles are basically advertisements for the drugs featured. Other ways members of the medical community are influenced include conferences sponsored by pharmaceutical companies and, of course, through the wide distribution of free drug samples (Drugwatch 2016).

The power of big pharma is most evident when it comes to regulating the cost of prescriptions drugs. Prescription drugs cost considerably more in the United States than anywhere else in the world. The pharmaceutical companies justify this expense by saying that the drugs cost so much because of how expensive it is to produce them. The industry claims that on average it costs $1.2 billion to produce a new drug, but an expert in the field says that the true cost is about $60 million (Light and Warburton 2011). The main reason that prescription drugs cost so much in the United States is that the U.S. government allows the pharmaceutical companies to set the prices for the drugs and also shields them from free-market competition. One CEO even went as far as raising the price of Daraprim, a drug used to treat toxoplasmosis, from $13.50 to $700 overnight. This exorbitant increase was reversed quickly due to public backlash (Malcolm and Szabo 2015). That was one victory for the public, but this is just one extreme example of an overpriced drug. There are many more overpriced drugs on the market. The situation has become so dire that 20% of patients do not get prescriptions filled or skip doses of their medication due to concerns about costs (Llamas 2014).

Mental Illness

Approximately 18% or 43.6 million U.S. adults suffer from mental illness annually (Center for Behavioral Health Statistics and Quality 2015). Recent data show a slight decline in incidence among adults, though social and economic costs associated with mental illness—suicide, divorce, substance abuse, domestic violence, unemployment and incalculable pain and mental anguish—remain high (Cockerham 2014). Mental illness is also common among children living in the United States. Approximately 20% (1 out of 5) children have a diagnosable mental disorder (Center for

Behavioral Health Statistics and Quality 2015). The most common disorders among children are attention-deficit/hyperactivity disorder (ADHD), mood disorders, and major depressive disorder. With the relationship between social factors and psychiatric features, mental disorders are an important area of study in the examination of social problems.

Criteria for mental illness involve the sociological concepts of norms, roles, social status, and behavior appropriate for social situations and settings (Cockerham 2014). Behavior categorized as "normal" is the standard for determining healthy thinking and behavior from a mental disorder. The difficulty in defining mental disorders is the ever-changing perspectives of society. For example, "homosexuality was considered a mental disorder by American psychiatrists until the early 1970s" (Cockerham 2014:3). Other terms and classifications have either been eliminated or evolved over time. Today, the American Psychiatric Association (2016) defines a mental illness as a "health condition involving changes in thinking, emotion or behavior."

TABLE 17

Prevalence of Any Mental Illness Among U.S. Adults (2014)

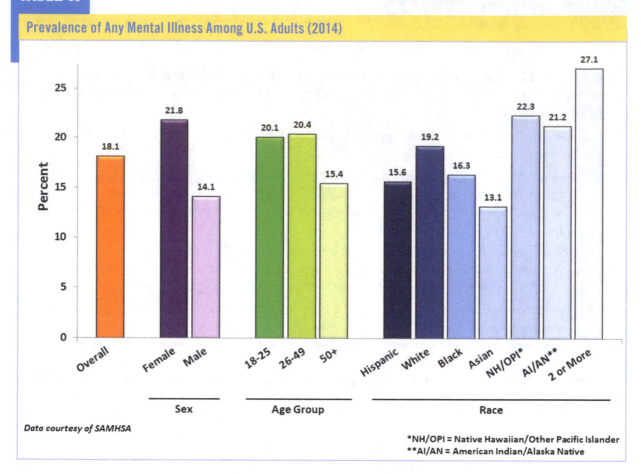

Data courtesy of SAMHSA

*NH/OPI = Native Hawaiian/Other Pacific Islander
**AI/AN = American Indian/Alaska Native

Data from the National Survey on Drug Use and Health (NSDUH) found approximately 4.2% or 9.2 million U.S. adults diagnosed currently or within the last year have serious functional impairment interfering or limiting one or more major life activities (Center for Behavioral Health Statistics and Quality 2015). Research studies have shown low-income people have the greatest prevalence of general mental disorders, schizophrenia, and personality disorders (Cockerham 2014). High prevalence rates among this population result from a lack of resources combined with stressful life conditions.

On average, only 13% of adults and 50% of children with a diagnosable mental illness receive help for a problem and only 50% of adults with a serious mental disorder receive treatment (Center for Behavioral Health Statistics and Quality 2015; CDC 2012). Of those individuals who seek out psychiatric care, research shows people go through a five stage decision-making process before accessing care (Cockerham 2014). First, people evaluate whether they have a real problem. Second, they discuss the problem with friends and relatives. Third, people evaluate whether they can deal with the problem on their own or if they need professional help. Fourth, they evaluate the type of help they need and are willing to utilize. Lastly, people decide which professional they will see for help.

There are times when an individual is involuntarily admitted to psychiatric treatment. Law enforcement and emergency personal are responsible for apprehending people under certain conditions. Apprehensions are usually made when people (1) attempt suicide, (2) demonstrate

Any Disorder

Lifetime Prevalence of 13 to 18 year olds

- **Lifetime Prevalence:** 46.3% of 13 to 18 year olds
- **Lifetime Prevalence of "Severe" Disorder:** 21.4% of 13 to 18 year olds have a "severe" disorder

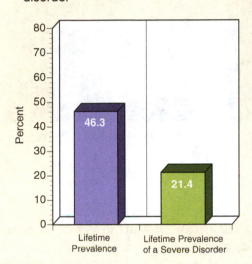

Demographics (for lifetime prevalence)

- **Sex:** Not statistically different
- **Age:** Statistically different

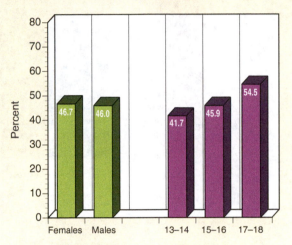

- **Race:** Statistically significant differences were found between non-Hispanic whites and other races

Merikangas KR, He J, Burstein M, Swanson SA, Avenevoli S, Cui L, Benjet C, Georgiades K, Swendsen J. Lifetime prevalence of mental disorders in U.S. adolescents: Results from the National Comorbidity Study-Adolescent Supplement (NCS-A). *J Am Acad Child Adolesc Psychiatry.* 2010 Oct;49(10):980-989.

Mental Health Service Use/Treatment Among U.S. Adults (2004–2008)

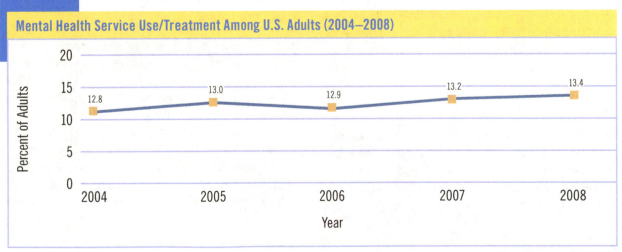

Data Courtesy of SAMHSA

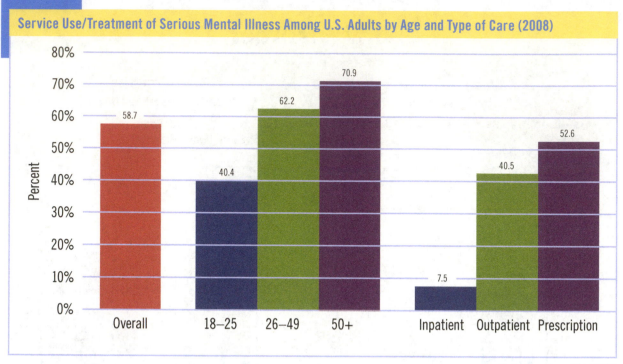

TABLE 20

Service Use/Treatment of Serious Mental Illness Among U.S. Adults by Age and Type of Care (2008)

Data Courtesy of SAMHSA

severely disordered behavior, (3) commit or threaten violence, (4) become a public nuisance or demonstrate harmful behavior, or (5) have a complaint filed against them by someone directly involved with them (Cockerham 2014). Data from the Department of Justice's *Survey of Inmates in State and Federal Correctional Facilities* and *Survey of Inmates in Local Jails* show local jails have the highest prevalence of mental problems among inmates at approximately 64.2% (U.S. Department of Justice 2002; 2004). This data also indicates fewer than half of inmates with mental illness have ever received treatment for their problem.

End-of-Life Issues

Over the last 100 years, medical care has become increasingly more effective and people are living longer (Hanneman 1999). However, advances in health care have consequences on social life. Though life expectancy is increasing, people are more likely to live longer with age-related diseases such as cancer, heart disease, and pulmonary disease (Hanneman 1999). This increase of the aging population living with a terminal illness has serious economic and social implications. Debates persist about the high, long-term costs of health care for the elderly as well as the daily care for those unable to live independently. Both these issues impose strain on families who find themselves responsible for the care of their aging loved ones.

Families often find themselves confronted in the position of caring for loved ones at home or sending their family member to live in a residential or assisted living facility. Either choice places financial and social demands on the family unit. Home hospice care is the most cost effective care available for end-of-life patients, but is one of the highest Medicare associated costs annually. Medicare associated costs for beneficiaries with at least one day of hospice from 2005–2011 were

TABLE 21

Sociodemographic Characteristics of the National Comorbidity Survey-Adolescent Supplement (NCS-A) (N=10,123)

Sociodemographic Characteristics	Category	N	Weighted %
Sex	Male	4,953	51.3
	Female	5,170	48.7
Age[a]	13–14	3,870	36.2
	15	1,887	20.5
	16	2,010	21.0
	17–18	2,356	22.3
Race	Non hispanic white	5,634	65.6
	Non hispanic black	1,953	15.1
	Hispanic	1,914	14.4
	Other	622	5.0
Parental Education	Less than high school	1,684	15.5
	High School	3,081	29.7
	Some college	1,998	19.4
	College grad	3,360	35.3
Parental Marital Status[b]	Married/cohabitating	4,602	78.6
	previous married	1,009	17.5
	never married	308	3.9
Poverty Index Ratio (PIR)	PIR ≤ 1.5 poor	1,717	14.7
	PIR ≤ 3.0	2,023	19.1
	PIR ≤ 6.0	3,101	31.9
	PIR > 6	3,282	34.3
Urbanicity	Metro	4,508	47.5
	Other urban	3,304	37.6
	Rural	2,311	14.9

Note: [a]weighted mean (SE) age = 15.2 (0.1); [b]other/unknown marital status are not presented

Source: Source: Sociodemographics Characteristics of the National Comorbidity Survey-Adolescent Supplement. http://www.ncbi.nlm.nih.gov/pmc/articles/PMC2946114

TABLE 22

Mental Health Treatment Among Prison/Jail Inmates

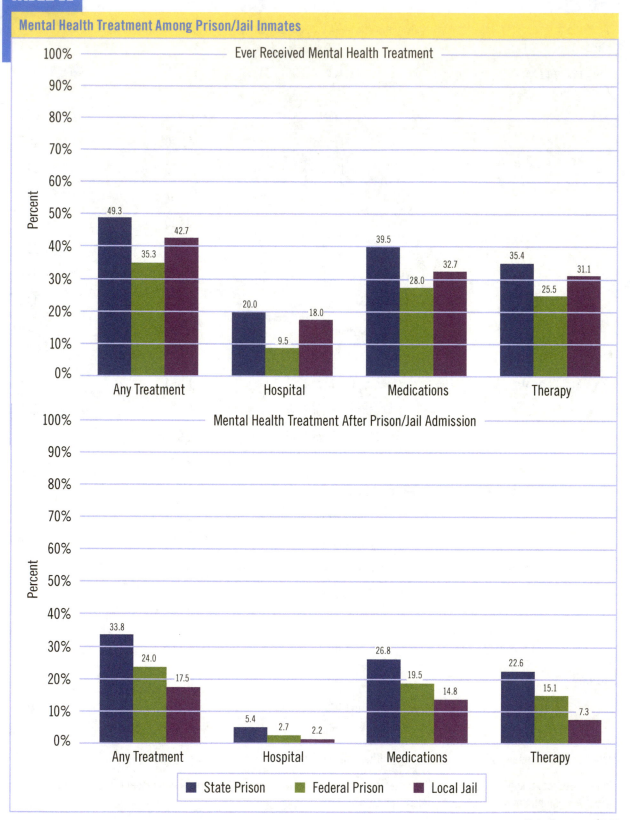

Ever Received Mental Health Treatment

Any Treatment: State Prison 49.3, Federal Prison 35.3, Local Jail 42.7
Hospital: State Prison 20.0, Federal Prison 9.5, Local Jail 18.0
Medications: State Prison 39.5, Federal Prison 28.0, Local Jail 32.7
Therapy: State Prison 35.4, Federal Prison 25.5, Local Jail 31.1

Mental Health Treatment After Prison/Jail Admission

Any Treatment: State Prison 33.8, Federal Prison 24.0, Local Jail 17.5
Hospital: State Prison 5.4, Federal Prison 2.7, Local Jail 2.2
Medications: State Prison 26.8, Federal Prison 19.5, Local Jail 14.8
Therapy: State Prison 22.6, Federal Prison 15.1, Local Jail 7.3

Legend: State Prison, Federal Prison, Local Jail

Data Courtesy of DOJ

Media and the Mentally Ill

It is common for media to highlight idiosyncrasies or characteristics of the mentally ill in television shows and movies. Consider some the fictional dramas you have viewed and how the mentally ill have been portrayed.

1. How do media outlets illustrate what it's like to live with a mental health condition? Describe the characters you have seen portrayed on television or in the movies and the how their conditions were depicted.

2. Do the images and descriptions of mental health conditions depicted on television and in the movies reinforce prejudice and discrimination or heighten awareness and promote acceptance? Explain.

3. Thinking about the data presented in this module about mental health and the demographics of the people managing mental health conditions, are the images and characteristics portrayed by the media about people with mental illness accurate? Provide supporting evidence to justify your perspective.

4. What role could the media play in changing the social conditions of the mentally ill? Do you think the media should play a role in improving the awareness and treatment of people with mental health conditions? Support your conclusions and recommendations with valid and reliable evidence.

approximately $10,000 per patient (Center for Medicaid and Medicare Services 2012).

Another social issue concerning people with terminal illnesses is the freedom to make end-of-life decisions including the type of care received (e.g., home hospice, skilled nursing facility, residential inpatient, etc.) and/or physician-assisted suicide options. In 1997, Oregon became the first state in the United States to legalize physician-assisted suicide known as the Death with Dignity Act. Each year, the state collects data about the patients and physicians who participate in legal physician-assisted suicide. Data shows people choose physician-assisted suicide for concerns about their loss of autonomy, decreasing ability to participate in life activities, and loss of dignity, not because they are disproportionately poor, less educated, or lack insurance coverage or access to hospice care (Oregon Public Health Division 2015). Oregon, Washington, Vermont, and California now have all passed Death with Dignity laws which all require participants to be diagnosed with a terminal illness and include a number of safeguards and controls to ensure participants are acting under sound mind and of their own free will and physicians are abiding by medical compliance procedures.

Evaluating Critical Thinking and Credibility

This module focuses on the concept of wellness and the struggle for equity in quality of life. People do not always consider health a human right and there is great controversy over who bears the responsibility of caring for one another. In life's pursuits, we often ignore the inequities in physical, mental, and social health until we are directly impacted by its consequences.

1. Reflect back on the social issues presented in this module.

2. Describe the emotional impact of sickness and the social and economic costs of illness.

TABLE 23

Proportion of Total Costs by Cost Center Grouping and Average Total Costs per Patient								
Cost Center Group	**2004**	**2005**	**2006**	**2007**	**2008**	**2009**	**2010**	**2011**
Total Costs by Cost Center Group Over All Providers								
Visiting services	61%	62%	63%	65%	65%	65%	66%	66%
Other services	23%	22%	21%	20%	20%	20%	20%	19%
Inpatient services	12%	13%	12%	11%	11%	11%	12%	12%
Non-reimbursable services	4%	4%	4%	4%	4%	4%	3%	3%
Total costs per patient over all providers (2010 dollars)	*$10,509*	*$10,522*	*$11,053*	*$11,544*	*$11,259*	*$11,243*	*$10,775*	*$10,710*
Total Costs by Cost Center Group Over at Provider Level								
Visiting services	65%	67%	67%	69%	70%	70%	70%	71%
Other services	24%	23%	23%	22%	21%	21%	21%	21%
Inpatient services	7%	7%	7%	7%	6%	7%	6%	6%
Non-reimbursable services	4%	3%	3%	3%	3%	3%	2%	2%
Median of providers' average costs per patient (2010 dollars)	*$10,510*	*$11,084*	*$11,216*	*$11,560*	*$11,103*	*$11,209*	*$10,822*	*$10,819*

*Costs per patient are in 2010 dollars, normalized using the hospital market basket update

3. Discuss the ethical responsibility of ensuring the physical, mental, and social wellness of all members of our society.

4. Analyze and explain which evidence presented in this module justifies the need for a healthy society.

Theoretical Analysis

In each module, we have discussed the application of theoretical paradigms to help us analyze and evaluate the social world around us. For this exercise, choose one of the following social problems presented in the module:

- Obesity
- Tobacco
- Big Pharma
- Mental Illness
- End of Life Issues

In the grid on the following page, explain the social issue and its impact on society and then analyze the problem using the six theoretical paradigms. Provide specific examples from the module to justify your theoretical analysis.

Summary of the Problem	

Impacts of the Problem (e.g. economic, environmental, biological, psychological, and social impacts.)	

Theory	Analysis
Macrosociology • Systems, institutions, processes, and procedures	
Functionalism • Purpose, contribution, and connections of social structures	
Confilct Theory • Power struggle between competing groups	
Feminism • Lives and experiences of women and minorities	
Environmental Theory • Adaptation or evolution of social structure in response to the physical and/or social environment	
Microsociology • Social interactions of individuals in everyday life	
Interactionism • Meaning or interpretation of words and symbols	
Exchange Theory • Motivation or self-interest of individuals	

Social Policy

Social policy is about changing economic, political, or social processes for the welfare of individuals in society by reducing inequalities (Vargas-Hernandez, Noruzi, and Ali 2011). Many people are working together to eliminate social inequality and improve the quality of life in our communities. Consider the physical and mental health issues discussed in this module and generate a list of legislative changes being deliberated locally, statewide, or nationally to increase health and wellness among individuals.

©Tefi/Shutterstock.com

1. Identify at least one new policy being proposed to address a social issue related to physical, mental, or social wellness?
2. How does the policy translate social values into operations for social change?

Physical, Mental, and Social Wellness   123

3. How will the policy ensure compliance with the law (both organizational and individual obedience)?

4. How will approval of the new law guide and improve thinking and behavior of individuals to increase wellness?

Social Movements and Reform

Each of the social issues presented in this module has a variety of groups working to change, reform, or address the problem. Successful social movements require a structure and organization to ensure the group's message is clear, membership is developed, and financial and other resources are garnered to sustain operations. The following groups are working toward social transformation on some of the issues presented in this module.

- Shape Up America (http://shapeup.org/)
- Mental Health America (http://www.mentalhealthamerica.net/)
- Death with Dignity (https://www.deathwithdignity.org/)
- Physicians for a National Health Program (http://www.pnhp.org/)

Research and investigate each organization to assess the impact they are having on the social issue they are addressing.

1. What is the goal of the organization?
2. What is the history of the organization?
3. How many members are involved in their organization?
4. What is the process for joining the organization?

©Tefi/Shutterstock.com

5. What support does the organization receive (e.g., grants, donations, volunteers, etc.)?

6. Who provides financial and other support to the organization?

7. What success in social transformation has the organization demonstrated to date? Explain the group's achievements and/or challenges to success.

8. Identify any groups or movements in your community addressing the social problems presented in this module.

References

American Psychiatric Association. 2016. "What is Mental Illness?" Retrieved February 12, 2016 (http://www.psychiatry.org/patients-families/what-is-mental-illness).

Centers for Disease Control and Prevention (CDC). 2016. "Current Cigarette Smoking Among Adults in the United States." National Center for Chronic Disease Prevention and Health Promotion. Office on Smoking and Health. Retrieved June 25, 2016. (http://www.cdc.gov/tobacco/data_statistics/fact_sheets/adult_data/cig_smoking/).

Centers for Disease Control and Prevention (CDC). 2016. "Youth and Tobacco Use."National Center for Chronic Disease Prevention and Health Promotion. Office on Smoking and Health. Retrieved June 25, 2016. (http://www.cdc.gov/tobacco/data_statistics/fact_sheets/youth_data/tobacco_use/index.htm).

Center for Behavioral Health Statistics and Quality. 2015. *Behavioral Health Trends in the United States: Results from the 2014 National Survey on Drug Use and Health* (HHS Publication No. SMA 15-4927, NSDUH Series H-50). Retrieved February 12, 2016 (http://www.samhsa.gov/data/).

Centers for Disease Control and Prevention (CDC). 2012. National Center for Health Statistics (NCHS). National Health and Nutrition Examination Survey Data. Hyattsville, MD: U.S. Department of Health and Human Services, Centers for Disease Control and Prevention. Retrieved February 12, 2016 (http://www.cdc.gov/nchs/nhanes.htm).

Centers for Disease Control and Prevention (CDC). 2013. "CDC Health Disparities and Inequalities Report (CHDIR), United States, 2013" in *Morbidity and Mortality Weekly Report (MMWR) Supplement* 62(3):1–189. Retrieved February 26, 2016 (www.cdc.gov/minority-health/chdireport.html).

Centers for Disease Control and Prevention (CDC). 2015. Division of Nutrition, Physical Activity, and Obesity. National Center for Chronic Disease Prevention and Health Promotion. Atlanta, GA:

U.S. Department of Health and Human Services. Retrieved February 26, 2016 (www.cdc.gov/obesity/data/adult.html).

Center for Medicaid and Medicare Services. 2012. *Medicare Hospice Payment Reform: Hospice Study Technical Report.* (HHSM-502005-00018I). Retrieved February 13, 2016 (https://www.cms.gov/Medicare/Medicare-Fee-for-Service-Payment/Hospice/Downloads/Hospice-Study-Technical-Report-4-29-13.pdf).

Cockerham, William C. 2014. *Sociology of Mental Disorder.* 9th ed. Upper Saddle River, NJ: Prentice Hall.

Commonwealth Fund. 2015. "31 million People were Underinsured in 2014; Many Skipped Needed Health Care and Depleted Savings to Pay Medical Bills." Retrieved February 26, 2016 (www.commonwealthfund.org/publications/press-releases/2015/May/underinsurance-brief-release).

Drugwatch. 2016. "Big Pharma." Retrieved June 26, 2016 (https://www.drugwatch.com/manufacturer/).

Fischer Walker, Christa L., Jamie Perin, Martin J. Aryee, Cynthia Boschi-Pinto, and Robert E. Black. 2012. "Diarrhea Incidence in Low- and Middle-income Countries in 1990 and 2010: A Systematic Review. *BMC Public Health* 12:220.

Gold, Jenny. 2009. "The 'Underinsurance' Problem Explained." *Kaiser Health News.* Retrieved February 26, 2016 (www.khn.org/news/underinsured-explained).

Hanneman, Robert A. 1999. "Your Money or Your Life: Access to Medical Care as a Social Problem." Pp. 43–47 in *Reading between the Lines,* edited by A. Konradi and M Schmidt. New York: McGraw-Hill Companies, Inc.

Healthy People 2020. 2011. "Access to Health Services." Retrieved February 26, 2016 (www.healthypeople.gov/2020/leading-health-indicators/infographic/access-health-services).

Jacobs, Majorie. 1995. "From the First to the Last Ash: The History, Economics, and Hazards of Tobacco: A comprehensive Adult Basic Education Curriculum." Cambridge Tobacco Education Program, Cambridge Department of Human Services. Retrieved June 25, 2016 (http://healthliteracy.worlded.org/docs/tobacco/Unit1/3economics_of.html).

Light, Donald and Rebecca Warburton. 2011. "Demythologizing the high costs of pharmaceutical research." *Biosocieties.* Retrieved June 26, 2016 (http://www.pharmamyths.net/files/Biosocieties_2011_Myths_of_High_Drug_Research_Costs.pdf).

Llamas, Michelle. 2014. "Big Pharma Cashes in on Americans Paying (Higher) Prices for Prescription Drugs." News, Drug and Device Manufacturers, Drugwatch.com. Retrieved June 26, 2016 (https://www.drugwatch.com/2014/10/15/americans-pay-higher-prices-prescription-drugs/).

Madeley, John. 1999. *Big Business Poor Peoples: The Impact of Transnational Corporations on the World's Poor.* New York: Zed Books, Ltd.

Malcolm, Hadley and Liz Szabo. 2015. "Turing pharma CEO recedes from public after back-tracking on drug price hike." *USA Today*. Retrieved June 26, 2007 (http://www.usatoday.com/story/money/business/2015/09/23/turing-pharmaceuticals-ceo-martin-shkreli-will-lower-price-of-daraprim/72670124/).

National Institute of Diabetes and Digestive and Kidney Diseases (NIDDK). 2012. Overweight and Obesity Statistics. National Institutes of Health. Bethesda, MD: U.S. Department of Health and Human Services. Retrieved February 29, 2016 (www.niddk.nih.gov/health-information/health-statistics/PAGES/overweight-obesity-statistics.aspx).

Oregon Public Health Division. 2015. "Oregon Death with Dignity Act: 2015 Date Summary." Retrieved February 13, 2016 (http://public.health.oregon.gov/ProviderPartnerResources/EvaluationResearch/DeathwithDignityAct/Documents/year18.pdf).

"Overweight and Obesity." 2015. World Health Organization. Fact sheet Number 311. Retrieved June 26, 2016 (http://www.who.int/mediacentre/factsheets/fs311/en/).

U.S. Department of Justice. 2002. "Data Collection: Survey of Inmates in Local Jails (SILJ)." Bureau of Justice Statistics. Retrieved February 12, 2016 (http://www.bjs.gov/index.cfm?ty=dcdetail&iid=274).

U.S. Department of Justice. 2004. "Data Collection: Survey of Inmates in State Correctional Facilities (SISCF)." Bureau of Justice Statistics. Retrieved February 12, 2016 (http://www.bjs.gov/index.cfm?ty=dcdetail&iid=275).

Vargas-Hernandez, Jose, Mohammad Reza Noruzi, and Irani Farhad Nezhad Haj Ali. 2011. "What Is Policy, Social Policy and Social Policy Changing?" *International Journal of Business and Social Science* 2(10):287–291.

World Health Organization (WHO). 2013. "WHO Report on the Global Tobacco Epidemic: Enforcing Bans on Tobacco Advertising, Promotion and Sponsorship." Retrieved June 25, 2016 (http://apps.who.int/iris/bitstream/10665/85380/1/9789241505871_eng.pdf).

Do you know the terms?

Using the list provided below, create a personal dictionary of key terms and concepts presented in this module. Include the term, phonetic spelling (if needed), and definition in your own words. Next, provide a real world example of the term or concept based on your previous knowledge or new information you learned in this module to help re-enforce learning.

Big pharma	Macrosociology
Body mass index	Mental illness
Conflict theory	Microsociology
End-of-life issues	Morbidity
Environmental theory	Mortality
Exchange theory	Overweight
Feminism	Obese
Food deserts	Symbolic interactionism
Functionalism	Tobacco
Life expectancy	

Index

Supplemental Nutrition Assistance Program (SNAP), 56
Symbolic interactionism, paradigm of, 22, 24, 76

T

Tax evasion, 94
Teamwork, 10
Technology gap, 75
Terrorism, issue of, 84–85
    9/11 attacks, 84
    labeling terrorists, 84
    "lone wolf," 85
    right-wing terrorists, 85
    and war on terror, 84
Tobacco, 113–114
Tobacco industry, 113
Transgender, 44
    violence and hate crimes, 44, 46
Tyner, Artika R., 104

U

UN Convention on the Prevention and Punishment of Genocide, 85
Underclass individuals, 53
United States
    Federal Aviation Administration (FAA), 97
    Food Access and Environment, 57
Universal Declaration of Human Rights (UDHR), 13
Unmanned combat aerial vehicles (UCAVs), 96
    for domestic surveillance and commercial use, 97
    military success of, 97
Upward intergenerational mobility, 51

V

Victims of Trafficking and Violence Protection Act (2000), 91
Victims of Trafficking and Violence Protection Reauthorization Act (2013), 92
Violence and hate crimes, 44, 46
    victims' perceptions of offender bias in, 47

W

Wage discrimination, laws against, 49
War, declaration of, 82–83
War on drugs, 95
War on Poverty, 55
War on terror, 84
War Profiteering Prevention Act (2007), 69
War profiteers, 69–70
Weber, Max, 65
Wellness, concept of, 121
White collar crimes, 93–94
White privilege, 41
Women, Infants, and Children (WIC), 56
World Report on Violence against Children (2006), 82
World Systems Theory, 66

Y

Young, Michael, 53

CPSIA information can be obtained
at www.ICGtesting.com
Printed in the USA
LVHW060745300720
661862LV00001B/2

9 781465 287557